Love is an Everyday Thing

Start Loving

THE MIRACLE OF FORGIVING

Love is an Everyday Thing

Colleen Townsend Evans

Guideposts

Carmel, New York 10512

TO the three *Mimi*s in my life

Scripture quotations not otherwise identified are from 1 Corinthians 13 from LETTERS TO YOUNG CHURCHES by J. B. Phillips. © Macmillan Publishing Co., Inc., 1947, 1957.

Scripture quotations identified KJV are from the King James Version of the Bible.

Scripture quotations identified RSV are from the Revised Standard Version of the Bible, copyrighted 1946, 1952, © 1971 and 1973.

Scripture quotations identified LB are from The Living Bible, Copyright © 1971 by Tyndale House Publishers, Wheaton, Illinois 60187. All rights reserved.

Scripture quotations identified MOFFATT are from THE BIBLE: A NEW TRANSLATION by James Moffatt. Copyright 1954 by James A. R. Moffatt. By permission of Harper & Row, Publishers, Inc.

Excerpts reprinted from THE PROPHET, by Kahlil Gibran, with permission of the publisher, Alfred A. Knopf, Inc. Copyright 1923 by Kahlil Gibran; renewal copyright 1951 by Administrators C.T.A. of Kahlil Gibran Estate, and Mary G. Gibran.

Excerpts from "Could You Have Loved This Much?" by Bob Considine, *Guideposts* (January 1966) are Copyright 1959, 1966 by Guideposts Associates, Inc.

"The Penalty of Love" by S. R. Lysaght from POEMS is by permission of Macmillan London and Basingstoke.

Gratefully . . . .

In writing about love these past few months I have found myself thanking God, again and again, for those who have poured love into my cup. My mother, Stella, who first taught me that love and commitment are bound together . . . her husband, Jim, who came into our lives when I was grown and who has since then been a source of joy and affirmation in my life . . . Louie's family—his mother and father, sisters and brother and their spouses—the whole wonderful clan that I claim as "my family, too" . . . and then our own nuclear family—Louie and our four children . . . Dan, Tim, Andie, and Jim . . . who have given me such gifts of love that I can't even begin to say what I feel for them.

But that isn't all . . . as I have been "living with love," a big extended family crowds into my mind . . . the family we have found in the three congregations we have served—in Bel Air and La Jolla, California, and now at National Presbyterian Church in Washington, D.C. . . . People, too many to mention, who pour love into our lives until—well, my cup overflows!

In relation to the practical aspect of the writing of these pages, there are several very special people to whom I want to give special thanks . . . . the Business and Professional Women's

Guild at National Presbyterian Church, a sisterhood of loving women who let me try out some of these ideas on them and then encouraged me. . . . Laura and John Hobe—Laura for once again loaning me her editorial gifts, and John because he and Laura have such a good partnership I simply think of the two of them together. . . . Likewise Jeanine and Gene Arnold, who not only provided a quiet place to work, but also food for the body and friendship for the heart.

COLLEEN TOWNSEND EVANS
WASHINGTON, D.C.

Contents

I

The Ways of Love

This has been a special day . . . special because my husband and I found time . . . but I wonder, is time found or is it taken? Or perhaps made? Let me begin again. . . .

Today my husband and I *made* time for a long walk together. It's been a busy year . . . Louie so involved in a new, creative parish . . . and me? . . . well, I've been busy, too. The past few days we've both been mumbling about being *too* busy—reminding one another that the thing that turns good-busy into bad-busy is when we can no longer find quiet little chinks of time for each other. And so we made time (I've since learned that the meeting got along *fine* without us!) . . . we stopped our world, jumped off, and started walking, which is one of our favorite things.

What a time and place to walk! You see, it's spring in Washington, and it is breathtakingly beautiful . . . we just had to get out into it. We began doing strange things from the begining of April on, as the forsythia announced the coming of spring, the cherry blossoms burst open . . . and then the city became a ridiculous blaze of color with azaleas, dogwood, tulips, daffodils. It's almost too much beauty to take at one time . . . and we found ourselves *ooh*ing and *ahh*ing and praising God for His handiwork as we drove down the streets. A wonderfully free-spirited friend rolled down his car window

13

one morning and shouted (reverently) to the heavens, "You show-off!" Really, it's that lovely!

As you can guess, Louie and I have a bad case of spring fever—Washington style. . . . Falling in love with this city isn't being untrue to where we come from, because everyone has a stake in Washington. . . . We feel we belong here as well as someplace else because this city is part of all our lives . . . but even more rational people say that spring in Washington is something to experience—and we experience it best when we walk.

Today we walked along the C&O Canal . . . starting in the heat of the day . . . peeking over Great Falls, and then making our way south. The original charter for the canal was granted 150 years ago . . . and there are lovely spots with lovely-sounding names all along the way . . . Sycamore Island, Violets Lock. Yet today I was more fascinated by the people than by the geography or history, for there seemed to be so many loving people—or people in love—on the trail. Was it just that it was spring? Or that I was so pleased to spend these moments with *my* love? Was I projecting my feelings on everyone else?

I seemed to sense humanity and our commonness with our fellowman . . . our love for one another . . . the cords of brotherly love that held us together. . . . Young people with Afros, holding hands, old people with white hair and tennis shoes, arm in arm . . . a little child riding piggyback on a young bearded daddy . . . and people right in the middle, like us . . . all out soaking up the beauty of this day.

Sometimes we walked for a long way in silence . . . other times we linked arms and talked for a while . . . now and then we almost got lost from one another as we ventured into little paths and looked at new, intriguing things . . . and then we'd come back together. We walked until the sun was hidden by the trees, then on into the dusk. Finally it was so dark we were stumbling along the path, and we headed for home.

All the time my mind was whirling with thoughts of love . . . for this is the time of year that speaks to us of love. . . . But it was not romantic love that I was thinking of—much as I'm for it! It was another kind of love—what the Bible speaks of as *agape*, which is a love that goes beyond romance . . . beyond any human love . . . and beyond life itself. It is the love of God for man . . . and it is something we need every day of our lives. That is what this book is about.

Recently I reread some of Erich Fromm's books and found these interesting statements about love. . . . "Without love, humanity could not exist for a day." . . . "Do we refer to love as the mature answer to the problem of existence, or do we speak of those immature forms of love which may be called 'symbiotic union'?" (Erich Fromm chose the former definition.)

It seemed to me that these words apply to God's *agape* love, for this is the love that completes us, matures us, as persons. And it also seemed to me that the paragraph nestled in the middle of 1 Corinthians 13—the great "love chapter"—tells us how.

Paul urges us to desire "a more excellent way" (*see* 1 Corinthians 12:31 KJV) . . . to seek after it . . . and this is where I am now in my own life. I seek to become more mature, to be more fulfilled as a person, as a woman. I'm reading a lot about maturity in newspapers and books these days, and there are many how-to instructions. . . . But what I really feel I want is to be completed in God's way . . . and so I must learn this art, this discipline, for it isn't something that just happens. It's something we must work for and develop in our lives. Nor is it something we can do only when we're in the mood to be loving. . . . No, it is something we *must* be open to every day . . . every minute of our lives . . . if we are to know its transforming power. For this *agape* love that comes into our being, motivating what we do and how we do it, is a gift from God, but like a muscle (which is also a gift from God) it must be exercised regularly to function well. Yes . . . I have a feeling that there will be days when it will be strong in us; and days when it will be weak . . . but the more we use it, the more we live according to its dictates, the stronger its influence will become in our lives. Out of this great reservoir we will then be able to give to others and receive it from others in a beautiful exchange of living, holy love that is far more magnificent than anything we can experience in our human capacity.

My mind rambles. . . . How wonderful life would be if everyone—*everyone*—truly loved his brothers and sisters! How simple . . . yet love is not simple, it is complex. Or is it? Is it so simple that perhaps it only seems complex?

There are various kinds of love mentioned in the Greek New Testament . . . *phileo, eros,* and *agape*. Life has been good and I have known friends, so I well understand *phileo*—friendly love. *Eros*—romantic love—I have been blessed with in the most loving way through my husband. But it is this *agape* love that strikes a chord in me . . . that says, "There is more . . . search on . . . yield more." . . . "Let this love be in you which is in Christ Jesus."

Natural love—*phileo* and *eros*—is not enough, warm and real and human as it is. It is not putting down natural love to admit that it has boundaries, limits, barriers. To be what love promises to be when we see God's love for us reflected in the springtime newness of life, it must have God's help. *Agape* must be intertwined with natural love to make it work.

In the thirteenth chapter of First Corinthians *agape* is never used interchangeably with *phileo* and *eros*. . . . That passage describes only one kind of love—God's. In a paragraph in the center of the chapter, I find words that are at once poetic and practical. Paul does not try to define *agape* . . . rather he reveals its nature . . . what it is like and how it behaves . . . and this appeals to the practical side of me.

This letter was written many centuries ago . . . but we are not unlike the Corinthians to whom it was addressed. . . . I am a twentieth-century Corinthian . . . needing to know the ways of *agape* love . . . how it treats other people, how it works, how it transforms me, and gives me the power to live beyond my human limitations . . . and needing to learn from these words of Paul as he tells me to seek this love above all else. I find special meaning in *Letters to Young Churches,* part of the J. B. Phillips translation of the New Testament. And so I read the words again. . . .

I am inspired by their beauty, challenged by their implications . . . and finally I am sad as I realize the chasm that separates the truth of these words from the consistent actions and attitudes of my everyday life. But it is a sadness sweetened with hope. . . . I decide to explore this path . . . to study these words . . . to be open to receive the gift of understanding . . . to experience and express *agape* love in my life in a deeper, more constant way.

I am eager to begin. . . . Yes, I want to take another walk, this one along the areas in my life where I need to grow, to mature. "This love of which I speak." . . . I feel adventure in the air!

If you're at this point in your life, come along with me. Let's walk this way together. It's a beautiful day!

2

Have I Been Slow Enough,
Long Enough?

Whenever I think of her, I feel a smile coming on and my heart is strangely warmed. I have loved my friend for a long time, almost from the moment we met. That was many years ago, when both of us were newcomers in the motion picture industry. We were very young . . . and in a field which isn't exactly known as a hotbed of believers, we just naturally sought each other out. But that's where the similarity ends . . . and again the smile comes on.

I was a new Christian . . . eager to share my faith. My friend had been a Christian most of her life, and she was—a free spirit. Her language, her manners, were a bit shocking, and a few of the movies she appeared in offended some people. In fact, I've been told that our friendship was hard for some to understand. Our backgrounds . . . our life-styles, our friends, the way we worshiped and the people with whom we worshiped . . . were so different. We really didn't have much going for our relationship except for one thing: we both loved Christ and wanted to serve Him. Our spiritual vibrations were the same—and so were some of our basic human vibrations—and we were drawn together into a deep, lasting, undemanding friendship . . . a sisterhood.

My friend had a rough exterior, and when I got to know her better I understood why. She was brought up with brothers—all of them big, lovable, tough guys—and her family had been poor. Her language, the way she'd come up to a person and slap him on the back, and her openness were perfectly natural to her. Anything else would have been a put-on.

Because I was more conventional I suppose people expected me to be shocked when my friend expressed her faith in ways—and in words—I had never heard before. But I wasn't. What came through to me instead was my friend's love for God . . . so fresh, so genuine, and right from her heart. To me, she was—and is—unique.

She could serve God in ways that I couldn't. She could get to people I couldn't reach . . . addicts, homosexuals, people who felt out of place in the church. She was the kind of person who could walk up to a woman suffering from the pain of an abortion and put her arm around her and say, "C'mon, let's pray for you." She brought so many of these troubled people to Jesus.

But to some of the more sophisticated, "intellectual" Christians I suppose she seemed far-out . . . flamboyant. I remember one night when I attended a Bible-study group with a woman who just bristled from the moment she saw my friend. Then our study leader, a dynamic woman we all loved—we called her "Teacher"—came in and sat near us. When my friend stood up to welcome everyone, "Teacher" said, "Oh, she's such a darling!" Later the woman who came with me said that she was shamed into thinking, "Well, if she can feel that way about the girl, I can at least be more open-minded!" And she was. Given a little time, she learned to appreciate her as a person from the inside out. (Thank you, "Teacher.")

I used to be bothered by the way people judged her. They were so impatient . . . which made *me* impatient with *them*. What's more, they didn't go to her with their criticism . . . they came to me. I tried to tell them what my friend was like on the inside, and how clearly God's love flowed through her . . . but I hurt for her.

She became a star almost overnight, and suddenly she was news. Everything she did, everything she said got into the papers, and being the honest person she was, she spoke and behaved exactly as she always had. One day, in a burst of enthusiasm and in the presence of some reporters, she referred to God in terms that were highly unorthodox and enticingly quotable. That did it! Her remark was printed, quoted, and reacted to in newspapers and magazines all around the world. People who used to shake their heads about her began to point their fingers at her. Church people in particular felt she had been disrespectful and flippant . . . and those who were puzzled by our friendship came right out and said, "Well, what do you think of your friend *now?*"

I thought what I had always thought of her . . . that she was a generous, dedicated Christian who wanted to serve her Lord in every way she could. And if Jesus didn't object to the way she expressed her love, why should anyone else? I was pretty angry by then, because I knew my friend was getting some feedback about the incident . . . letters, telephone calls, glares, whispered remarks. But she seemed so calm, so untroubled by it all. She was the same warm, helpful, outgoing person I had always known. One day I simply had to ask her about it.

"How can you take it so quietly?" I said. "Doesn't it bother you when so many people criticize you?"

She smiled . . . more concerned with *my* distress than her own . . . and said, "Honey, I don't even see their prejudice—I just see them perfect!"

I felt tears in my eyes . . . and I can feel them now as I remember how patient she was. She was no theologian, but she *knew* God loved her and that made all the difference in her attitude. She was telling *me* to be more patient with her critics. Her attitude was teaching me to look at them through the eyes of God and see them as they could be—perfect—when God had more time to work within them. ("Please be patient with me—God isn't finished with me yet.") She was telling me that if I opened myself to God's love, instead of relying on my own human love, I would be much more patient with them while they were in the process of becoming mature Christians.

To me, that was beautiful . . . everyone was judging her, and she was judging no one. That's the way my friend is . . . and it's the way I want to be. . . .

Love is slow to lose patience . . . ah, yes, patience is some-thing I need every day—almost every minute—of my life. For I want things to be right, good, better, and happier *now*. And if not now, then tomorrow at the very latest! (Louie calls me his "fixer.") It seems to me that this is a natural way for love to behave.

Yet Paul is telling us that God's love—*agape*—is different, and sometimes that's hard for me to understand. There is so much that needs to be changed and healed and fixed in our world—surely God must want to get it done quickly. How can He be so patient? . . . That's what I need to find out. How?

How could Jesus be so patient with those who followed Him? Like all of us, they had their faults—some were pretty rough characters, too, others only a little smoother . . . they had their jealousies and snobberies . . . they let Him down more than once . . . sometimes they didn't pay attention to what He was saying. Yet He loved them most patiently, regardless of their merit or the cost to Him.

Perhaps Jesus saw things in them that other people couldn't —or wouldn't—see. Yes, there's a clue! Jesus always saw beyond the surface of a person . . . He looked at the inner core, at the motivation . . . He saw what each person could become. And this is what Paul is telling the Corinthians—and us—to do: to look beyond the outer roughness and facade of our brothers and sisters . . . to see them the way God sees you and me.

One of the Greek words for "patience" is *makrothumia* and it always means "patience with *people*." *Makro* means "big" or "deep," and *thumia* means "emotion" or "passion" . . . it describes a person who has been wronged and who could strike back—but choses not to do it. This is the word used to describe God Himself in His relationship to us . . . and this is the word Paul uses to spell out for the Corinthians the way God's love is expressed through us in everyday life: **Love is slow to lose patience with people** . . . even when it is wronged. Obviously this isn't always the way we behave toward one another . . . it's the way God behaves toward *us*. And only if we are open to His love for us can we express it to others.

In the Corinthian church there were people from many different backgrounds. Some were racy and uncouth, while others were sophisticated and proper . . . and Paul was urging the more polished believers to be patient with the rough ones. He was pointing out that while those rough ones were in the process of becoming new, they needed a lot of understanding. My daughter has just reminded me that today the reverse is also true. Her world—though not "Corinthian rough"—is certainly casual and relaxed . . . and Andie feels that she and her friends need patience and understanding for those who have been raised in the more proper, formal setting of the past.

We all begin our spiritual life at different points . . . and perhaps where we *are* is not as important as the direction in which we are headed. Beneath many of the rough exteriors in our midst are hearts that are open to God. There is so much we can learn from them.

Paul realized, I'm sure, that a rigid, judging attitude could squelch the life of the Spirit in a church, and so he urged the Corinthians to be more generous toward each other. Generous . . . there's another clue. . . . When love is patient, it gives of itself . . . it does not demand of others. And generosity is one of the most outstanding characteristics of Jesus and all who follow Him. "Love one another as I have loved you," He said (*see* John 13:34 KJV), and who can deny that Jesus has expressed endless patience and generosity in His love for us.

When we are impatient with people . . . when we demand a certain level of performance from them, we may turn away some of the finest people with whom God wants to bless our lives. I'm thinking of a couple we met several years back. Walter and Carol were young, loud, profane, defensive, cynical— and very much in need of the kind of love only God can give. Both had been married before—unhappily; they were living with the ghosts of their unhappy past. Carol had married her childhood sweetheart when she was sixteen, and after several years of trying very hard to make the marriage work she decided that she wanted a divorce. By that time she was nineteen, and very bitter. Her language had become coarse and hard—which was the way she felt inside—and she was suspicious of anyone who was nice to her. The only exception was Walter, whom she met a few years later. Together they seemed to hold the world at arm's length.

When Walter and Carol had been married a year they went shopping for a church—Sunday services were a habit from childhood, nothing more. But when they walked through the doors of church for the first time—together—something happened to them. They were surrounded by love—*God's* love—moving through the congregation. They found some other young couples—or rather, some other young couples found *them*—and no one paid any attention to their rough speech. It didn't matter whether they distrusted the gestures of friendship—the gestures were given anyway, over and over. And if they declined an invitation to join a group or serve on a committee, they were invited again. Gradually they began responding. They came back each Sunday, and bit by bit they began to serve. They had a fine sense of what people needed and wanted from the church, and as they began to suggest new programs we found their ideas were met with enthusiasm from the congregation. And, most wonderful of all, their lives began to reflect the change that was going on inside them—God's love was warming them, breaking down their defenses, overcoming their fear and distrust of people. We could actually see the new life growing up beside the old one, and I'll never forget the way they described how much Jesus meant to them in words that wouldn't look well in print—but that thrilled us because they were so truly from the heart!

Oh, Lord, I'm glad you brought Walter and Carol to us. . . . The truth is, we needed them more than they needed us!

In some translations I've read the phrase, "Love is patient and kind," and I've wondered why the word *kindness* was linked with *patience*. Isn't patience enough?

Perhaps not, at least in some circumstances. . . . I'll have to try it out in my everyday life. Let's see . . . when love prompts me to be patient, that could mean that I'm passive. I might be holding something back—an impulse, a thoughtless remark. Anyway, something is going on *inside* me . . . that's where the action is. But when love prompts me to be kind, that means I must *do* something. I must act and not hold back. The action is *outside* me . . . reaching into the lives of others. Yes, now I can see the reason for this particular translation, and I've learned something from it. When we love Jesus, we don't keep our feelings bottled up inside us. . . . We express our love in acts of kindness. We do something about it.

When we are kind, we are expressing our patience in ways others can understand. For instance, when someone is pseudopatient and just puts up with me, I feel put down, left out—but when someone gives me a smile, or a friendly word, or a hand-clasp that says, "I am your sister—your brother," I feel loved, included . . . not just endured. I am touched by that person's patience. These little tokens are like tiny stones dropped into a lake . . . the ripples growing, never exhausting themselves.

Kindness can cost us nothing—or it can cost us dearly if we don't express it. I remember the sadness in the face of a fine old gentleman who told me how he lost his wife because he wasn't patient enough—and kind enough—when she needed him. Some years before I met him his wife had begun to worry about getting older. She fussed over her appearance and tried to look younger by dressing in ways that, to him, seemed foolish, even embarrassing. "It was pride, I guess, that got in my way," he said. "I kept wondering what people were thinking of me. I tried to be patient, but I never thought of being kind to her. And after all, she was going through a difficult time." Impatience won out, and he got a divorce. But if only he had waited . . . if only he had let her know that he *could* wait . . . because in time his former wife seemed to mature most beautifully and became a wonderful, helpful, responsible person. Several years later, when she died, her friends told him that she died of a broken heart. "There seemed to be no other cause of death," he said.

And I know of another couple whose happiness might have been saved by a little kindness . . . a little stretching. They were a young minister and his wife whose parish was a small country town where life was very simple. Doreen was a wonderful wife—extremely devoted to Dwight and his ministry. She played the piano for all the church services, attended the women's group, taught a Sunday-school class and visited as many shut-ins as she could . . . not because she had to, but because she wanted to. And then Dwight was called to a church in a large city. The people in their new congregation were wealthy and bright, and, as Dwight began associating with them, he changed. His interests broadened and he began to outgrow his wife mentally and emotionally. Doreen was a bright girl, and she could see what was happening to their marriage, so she began to follow the advice in one of Dwight's sermons—"Be the Real You." She read more widely, and talked to more people, and she found out what was going on in the world around her. In other words, Doreen came out of her shell. But she needed encouragement . . . she needed someone to say, "Look, this is an exciting change in our lives—let's not be afraid of it. . . . I want you to be who you really are. Here, let me help you—go ahead and make mistakes—that's how we learn." But that isn't what happened. Instead of being pleased with the change in his wife, Dwight felt threatened by it. He was impatient with Doreen. He criticized her when she made mistakes and she began to feel awkward, unsure of herself. Yet the kindness and patience of others convinced her that she was going in the right direction. Finally, she made her choice—she was going to be herself in spite of her husband. A year later they were divorced.

Human love is so quick to lose patience . . . so blind to the need for kindness in others. But how different it can be when we allow God to love through us.

Our friend Jenny knew her husband was in trouble long before the authorities knocked on their door. While she didn't know what he had done, she knew that he wasn't the same man anymore. He worked late every night. He was irritable with her and the children, defensive when she asked, "Honey, what's the matter?" Sometimes she was hurt by his abruptness, and wanted to hurt back . . . but she didn't. She waited as long as she could and when she felt her patience running out she asked God to help her, to be patient *for* her. And He did. Jenny says she doesn't know quite what happened, but all of a sudden she was calm, tender, quietly sympathetic in spite of what her husband did or said. She realized that there were ways in which she could express what she felt . . . . she could tell her husband that she loved him by being kind . . . in the countless little ways that are so important to any marriage. Because she could feel his pain, she wanted him to feel her comfort . . . and apparently he did. Then one day Jenny learned through the morning newspaper the details of her husband's involvement in a complicated network of embezzlement. But instead of confronting him with his wrongdoing, Jenny felt a tremendous peace sweeping through her. Now she could understand why her husband had changed, why he had been so tormented. She didn't need to tell him—he knew he was wrong, and he wanted to make amends for what he had done. And he did. Although he knew he might be sentenced to prison, he freed himself from the burden of guilt he had been carrying for many months. Jenny's patient love had reached him and in the months and years that followed, that same love helped him become part of his family again.

It helps me to know that God's love is *slow* to lose patience. . . . That brings it within my reach. If this love were perfectly patient, or if it *never* lost patience, I don't know what I'd do! We should be patient with people—but there are times when we should *not* be. There are times when love must express itself in *impatience*. Even Jesus lost patience with some people—the I'm-always-right types, the ones who were always judging others. I think we *should* be impatient with injustice, with greed, with hatred. We should be impatient when one of God's children continues to hurt another. We should be impatient when we are used in a way that is neither helpful nor healthy for others or for ourselves.

To bring it down to everyday life, we should be impatient with members of our own family when they are inconsiderate of others in the family. And, let's be honest, there are times when the family has to come down hard and be impatient with us!

In our family we have two cars (with five licensed drivers, we can't make it with one, in spite of our ecological concern). Each of us, with the exception of my husband, used to have the bad habit of pulling into the driveway and parking right in the middle. And then, when Louie came home in the second car, he couldn't get into the driveway.

For years I was the only other driver in the family, and I must say he was very patient with me. But when our children seemed to be picking up their mother's bad habit, Louie's patience began to wear thin. One day he pronounced an ultimatum —he was still patient, but *very* firm: the next time the driveway was blocked, the guilty party would have to go out—rain, sleet, or snow—and repark both cars. Period! There was going to be a little discipline in our family.

A few days later Louie walked in, cold and b-r-ry from the winter weather, but more than a little warmed by the heat that was rising from his collar. "Okay," he said, "who did it this time?"

The whole family was there, plus a houseguest, and all eyes turned on me. That's right—*guess who* had used the car last, and everyone knew it! Such a silly thing, but there was plenty of *ouch!* in it. It was hard for me to get up and take my medicine . . . it was hard to be humbled in front of a guest . . . and it was *very* hard to be nice to my husband at dinner. *But*—I haven't parked in the middle of the driveway since . . . and although my little lesson has become a family funny, I think the other drivers have learned from it, too. What's more important, we all realized that Louie had to become impatient with us to be really loving to us.

I realize that this incident seems like a minor one compared to some of the larger areas of life . . . but I think we need patience in the little everyday areas of irritation as well. . . . Perhaps *there* most of all, for so many times in each day we need to know whether to have or to lose patience with unmade beds, dirty bathtubs, toothpaste tubes squeezed the wrong way (not *our* way!)—and cars parked in the middle of the driveway.

Love is slow to lose patience . . . yes, but how slow? For how long? What about people who try our patience? We all know people like that, and sometimes it's hard to decide when we've been slow enough, long enough. Only now and then does the signal come through clearly, unexpectedly—and we just *know*. It was that way for me one afternoon when I received a call from a woman we had known for a long time. She had a drug problem —in her case it was alcohol—and whenever she got high she'd call us up. Since I was home most often I usually was the one who listened to her complaints. When she was sober, she was a fine, lovable person, but when she was drinking she was abusive, manipulative. I had tried to be patient with her because she needed love so badly and I wanted her to know she had mine. But on that particular afternoon I felt she was trying to use me in a new way which had nothing to do with love. She was furious about something her husband had done, and she tried to make me say something against him—or to agree with her by not saying anything. Now, to me, that's tops in the dirty-tricks department, and something in me said, "That's it!" Suddenly I knew I'd been slow enough, long enough—and I wasn't very loving to allow her to do this to me or to anyone else. I don't remember my exact words (perhaps because my heart was pounding so loud that I couldn't hear them), but I told her in quite certain terms that I didn't like what she was doing to her husband, to herself,

or to me. I said I would like to see her or hear from her any-
time she had something to say, but not to call us anymore when
she was in the mood to be abusive. And—bang!—I hung up!

My children stood amazed, because I usually don't behave that
way, and then all four of them broke out in applause. "Yea,
Mom! Atta girl!" they cheered, so I guess they sensed that I had
been slow enough, long enough, before I did.

There were no more abusive calls, and when I saw the woman
in church the next Sunday there was something different about
our relationship. Actually I thought it might have ended, but it
didn't. We never mentioned her last call, but I knew she remembered it, and I felt she was allowing me to get closer to her than
I had ever been. She seemed to understand that I had to lose
patience with her because I loved her . . . and *because* I loved
her I had to let her know I felt she was hurting herself—and
trying to manipulate me.

To lie down and take anything in the name of love is not
right, for injustice harms the giver as well as the receiver. And
sometimes groups of people must say to those who are holding
them down and exploiting them, "Because we love God, and
love you, and love ourselves, we cannot let you do this to us."

When we lose patience, that doesn't mean that we have to
abandon love or give in to hate. Human love may not be able to
make that distinction, but God's love can. . . . He can lose
patience lovingly.

I think the Black Movement is an example of people who had
reason to lose patience . . . and now it's the Establishment's
turn to understand their impatience. If it were *my* children
going to inferior schools . . . if *my* family had to live in
crowded, dilapidated buildings . . . if *my* husband couldn't get
a job in the field of his choice, and if he couldn't even get the
training he needed to do the job—I don't know if I would have
been as patient. And so, when our black friends sometimes express hostility toward us, even though many of us have (in our
fumbling way) tried to do something to correct the wrongs done
to them, we have to remind ourselves of what they've suffered . . . and for how long.

At times, while working on a project with a black person, I
can feel this hostility, and I think, "Why *me?* I'm in your corner!" But then I think, "Wait a minute—what I'm getting from

them, they've taken for three hundred years . . . a hundred times over."

While it's comforting to know that love sometimes needs to express itself through impatience, my great need is to learn the lesson that Paul is teaching us in this verse. For if anything makes me quick to lose patience, it is the impatience of others . . . and this is the area where I must try harder to let God take over for me. I always have an easier time being patient with a person or a group who are fighting their way up than with those who are on top. Perhaps if I see that people are moving in a loving direction, I can be less demanding of them. But if I see that they're not moving at all—or moving away from God's love —well, perhaps then I must try to be honest with them about the way I feel. Honest, but not impatient . . . speaking the truth, but in love . . . yes, that will be difficult for me. But not for God!

Jesus, it's just amazing how loving and patient You are with me. So when I'm about to lose my patience with someone—when I haven't been slow enough, long enough, let me remember Your wonderful example. May it inspire me to ask less of others who are also walking the Way, and to give more of myself . . . to be more than I am . . . to love more than I can—and as much as You can. Amen.

3

This love . . . looks for a way of being constructive . . . .

Can I Help You?

One of the most beautiful women I have ever known was my husband's grandmother. When I first met her she was almost ninety years old . . . tiny, fragile, with one of the most elegantly boned faces I've ever seen. But at ninety it's not your face or your frame that counts. It's your soul . . . the way you've lived, the feelings you've known, the thoughts that have passed through your mind. They're what show. And Grandmother Egly's beauty came from deep inside her.

I can picture her now the way she was when I first saw her . . . sitting in the kitchen, which was the busiest place in the house, darning a sock for someone. And as any of the family members passed by, she would look up and say, "And what can I do for *you* today?" This was not just a chance remark—it was the theme of her life.

When I think of love being constructive, I think of Grandmother Egly. She didn't just sit back, waiting for someone's need to fall into her lap. She was eager to love . . . she wanted to help . . . and she looked for the things that needed doing. This is the way Paul describes God's love for us, and he urges the Corinthians—and us—to let this love work its way through us and into the lives of others. Too often human love says, "You got yourself into this, now get yourself out!" . . . "Help your-

30

self!" . . . "You can do it if you try." God's love knows no such limitations. It is love on the offensive . . . love offering itself, not waiting to be asked. It asks, "What can I do for *you* today?"

Love looks for a way of being constructive . . . that means love is original, creative, resourceful. It thinks of things that haven't been done before, things that are missing from someone's life. It reaches into its own being to find what is needed to fill the emptiness. It heals.

A very busy woman I know took time to do something wonderfully creative for a friend whose house had just been sold. Michelle's friend was expecting a visit from the buyer's wife—who was seeing the house for the first time—when she suddenly was called out of town. In her absence Michelle offered to show the house to the new owner—and she did far more than that. She wanted the buyer's wife to feel warm and comfortable when she saw her new home for the first time . . . and knowing that her friend had no time to pick up around the house before she left, she went there ahead of time and straightened up. Then, because she had read somewhere that people feel at home in a house when they smell something good cooking in the oven, Michelle baked some gingerbread. Now, I never would have thought of that!

I know that I can't be very original on my own. I need help . . . I need God's constructive touch in my life before I can be of real assistance to someone else.

For instance, I have always wanted to be like Grandmother Egly . . . right in the middle of my family, doing things for them. . . . Not necessarily big things, but the little things that have so much meaning and are often bypassed in our busy lives. How much I have wanted to love my family actively, eagerly, creatively, particularly since our move to Washington, the city of daily fascinating events . . . but there has been the problem of time. On almost any day I wouldn't have dared ask my husband and children, "What can I do for you today?" They might have told me and I would have had to say, "Sorry—too busy" . . . too busy doing other things, all of them important and interesting. Yet I missed my time with my family . . . I resented the demanding, fascinating events and duties that kept me from them. I wanted to *love* the people I love!

Love takes time . . . perhaps that's what Paul is telling us when he uses the word *constructive*. We can't be original or creative if we don't take the time to do what needs doing. We can't help someone if we don't have a moment to spare. . . . And whoever heard of a need waiting in line or fitting into a schedule?

And so, there, in the midst of my heavily trafficked life, God said to me, "And what can I do for you today?" He did it through a friend who sensed the tension that was building up inside me. One day she said, "Coke, if you need time, you must *make* time. . . . Keep a part of each week for yourself, and then do whatever you want with it." It seemed impossible at first, but I knew I had to try. I had to create time . . . which meant that I had to be constructive in my own life. I had to begin getting my schedule from God—who knows my real needs—and not from other people, however well meaning they might be.

I began setting aside two days a week when I make no appointments unless something really urgent must be done. Then I do the things I really want to do for my family and friends . . . and sometimes just for myself. I read, I pray, I write, I cook a pot of soup for a sick friend—and mostly just make myself available to those I love. Now, on these two days each week, I can say to my family, "Hey, you guys, what can I do for you today?" . . . and really *mean* it!

If I seem to be making a case for a woman being a slave to her family—jumping to their every whim, making them totally dependent on her—well, I'm not. I believe strongly that a woman ought to have her own things to do while "looking well to the ways of her household" (*see* Proverbs 31:27 KJV). But there is a difference between a spineless slave and a woman who can sense her family's needs and offer them some creative love.

Let's not forget, though . . . when Paul says that love is constructive, helpful, healing, he is not speaking to women. . . . He is speaking to *people,* to men and women who are Christians, who want to be like Jesus in their daily lives. This *constructive* love is a gift God has for all of us, male and female alike . . . and of course, some people are more abandoned than others, more willing to receive the gift and let it function in their lives. I'm thinking of someone like my husband's mother, who may be the all-time make-the-crooked-places-straight person in my life. Her sensitivity is truly a gift, and through the years I have watched in amazement as she was helpful in ways that never would have occurred to me.

Many years ago, in a situation that was so typical of her, Mother Evans helped her husband do something that seemed impossible. Louie's father was a busy pastor of a church that was always packed full. He also kept adding appointments to his little engagement book, and sometimes it was difficult to find the time to do everything that had to be done.

Once there was a bind—"Near-panic would describe it more realistically," Mother Evans says—when Louie's father realized that he had to make two high-school commencement addresses on the same day, one in Glendale in the afternoon, and one in Santa Ana early in the evening. The schools were fifty miles apart, and in those days in California there weren't any free-ways—in fact, the freeways were then being built, which made traffic a nightmare. It was too late to make arrangements for another speaker, but was it possible for Daddy Evans to be in both places on time? Mother said she'd see what she could do.

She called an automobile club and asked them for the best route from one school to another. Yes, it just might be done . . . but perhaps not during rush hour, and that's when they had to travel. Mother Evans decided to try it out herself. On the day before the two addresses, and during the same hours they would have to travel, she made the trip—successfully, but with only seconds to spare.

The next day Mother waited for Daddy outside the Glendale High School—motor running and a lunch already packed for him to eat on the way. As soon as his address was finished, he left, got in the car, and off they went toward Santa Ana. They made it to the next school just as the processional line was beginning to move.

As Mother Evans describes it, "He left the car, robe flapping in the breeze as he strode across the lawn to find his place in the line. I could only breathe a sigh of gratitude. Once again, by the grace of God!"

Not all of us can be a Mother Evans. But I have learned something very beautiful from her example: *To love is to serve.* Whether you're a man or a woman, a very important part of loving is doing things for those you love. Just as Jesus took up the basin and the towel and washed the feet of His friends, we can serve those nearest our hearts by doing the little everyday things that they can't do for themselves. Love that is constructive makes time for the basin and the towel.

Love looks for a way of being constructive . . . not only in little ways, but in times of crisis and tragedy. How often, in the midst of heartbreak, we feel hopeless, overcome, totally helpless! And so we might remain if we were left to our own resources. But we aren't on our own, not if we don't wish to be. We have God's wonderful healing love, and once we open ourselves up to it . . . when we meet the pain and sorrow head-on, letting it wash through us, God's comfort will follow. That's when something amazing happens. Out of the tragedy grows something constructive—a blessing, not only in our lives, but in the lives of others.

I'm thinking of a couple we know and love who even now are going through not what I think of as tragedy but certainly deep trauma in their personal lives. But because they love God they feel Him at work even through strange and troubling events. We'll call them John and Jeannie Roberts.

John is a young investment man whose professional reputation and success stemmed from his ability to make wise and profitable investments. Over a number of years he developed a successful business relationship with a friend who was an importer. After a few years, when his confidence and trust in his friend had grown sufficiently, John raised over one million dollars from his family and a few friends to be invested in the importing business. One day some months later he was horrified to learn that his friend's business actually did not even exist. The funds of the family and friends were now lost, and he himself faced bankruptcy. His friend will go to jail, and John's career as it *had* existed was forever altered.

It was during this period of personal devastation and humiliation that John came to appreciate that it is not what happens in life that matters, but how we meet what happens. Both he and his wife felt God's love through their friends and their family who had lost so much and yet rallied around them, giving them the strength to cope with the legal and financial hurdles they faced. With this kind of support, and the prayers of many friends, John and his family were able to face up to their situation—so well, in fact, that his nine-year-old daughter could say, "Mommy has been so much happier ever since Daddy got poor."

A few years ago, two of our friends in the ministry, Jim and Virginia Angell, suffered a loss that really *was* a tragedy. For a long time I couldn't think of it without choking up. Their oldest daughter, Susan, a beautiful girl, was killed in an automobile accident. The tragedy came suddenly, unexpectedly, early one Easter morning. When we heard, our hearts went into mourning with them . . . their loss was so great. But God finds a way through the most terrible agonies, and He brings something good out of them. . . . Not that He replaces the loved one with someone or something else—that could never be . . . . nor does He wipe out the memory of the loving. . . . No, He simply brings something worthwhile out of the agony . . . something we can pass on to others. For the Angells it was a book—a beautiful book!—*O Susan,* written by Jim to help and comfort others who might someday mourn the loss of a person they loved. In it he describes the depth of their grief and the gradual, beautiful, wonderful healing of God's love. This is love looking for—and finding—a way of being constructive.

Love is homemade . . . and when we want to be helpful, it's best to begin doing it close up, with those who are nearest. But that's not all . . . if God's love is a growing part of our lives, He won't allow us to stop there. We are not only part of a family . . . we're part of the world.

When love is constructive, it cares about more than the *now* of life . . . it thinks about the future, and about those who will live on this earth after us. You might even say that love is ecology-minded!

This was brought home to me during the recent energy crisis. Winter had come to Washington and it was cold, not only outside but inside our house. Of course, we all had been warned about the approaching shortage . . . we were not without our prophets and they prepared us if we had ears to hear. In fact, we had one of these prophets in our own family, where it was impossible *not* to hear. And our son Dan has been good for us . . . encouraging us to sell a big car and buy a smaller one that goes twice as far on a tank of gas, urging us to move closer to our work and schools, keeping after us to recycle anything, everything . . . and when the fuel shortage came, turning our ther-

mostat down—wa-a-ay down—even though it meant dressing for
the inside as though we were outside. But there I sat—in long
woolen pants and layers of sweaters, wearing my husband's heavy
hiking socks—just ever so slightly proud of being slightly miserable and cold.

Our son cares about the generations to come. He isn't anxious
for tomorrow . . . he's looking for a way of being constructive.
And one of the most constructive things we all can do for the
future, he says, is to change the way we think about energy.
Almost always, the tools that run on power are convenience
items, and so we must begin to choose simplicity rather than
convenience whenever possible. . . . I can beat cream by hand
instead of with a mixer. I can use an ordinary toothbrush rather
than an electric one. I can walk more often—which I love to do
—even ride a bicycle instead of using the car every time I go
somewhere. Yes, when you really think about it, simplicity can
be very helpful.

A constructive attitude can be helpful, too, especially when
we can't do anything about a particular situation. . . . I'm
thinking of the fuel shortage and the long lines of cars at the
gas stations. One friend, who waited for an unusually long time,
grumbling all the way, was thoroughly frustrated when I saw
her. Another friend waited just as long, but took a book to read
. . . no energy lost there. So when my gas gauge told me it was
my turn to wait it out, I felt very constructive (and a little bit
smug) as I got in the car, carrying a good book under my arm.
Unfortunately, as I discovered after I was already in line, I forgot my glasses, and I can't read a word without them. Oh, well,
I tried. . . .

Maybe trying—or wanting to try—is the most important part
of constructive love. We won't always find a way to help, nor will
our help always meet the need, but with God's *agape* love at
work in us, we will always be looking for a way to serve.

Sometimes we come upon a need quite suddenly, one that has
been there all along, but of which we weren't aware. Most of the
time we're caught up in our family life and community problems, and we may forget about the world out there . . . until
God pricks our conscience and keeps us awake at night.

Recently Louie and I attended a farewell dinner party for two
friends who were leaving Washington to become U.S. ambassa-

dors to a new, young nation—one that belongs to the emerging Third World, as it is called. I learned a lot that night . . . I was seated at a table with several Third World leaders and I felt like an eager sponge as I listened while they spoke of their concern for the problems in their native lands. They serve the *have-not* countries of the world today . . . countries where survival is a daily struggle with disease, famine, ignorance, filth, and desperate longing. These men and women, these representatives of their governments, commute regularly between the *have* and the *have-not* nations, so they know how very far their countries must go to catch up. And it isn't just a matter of catching up . . . the very existence of these nations depends upon their ability to support themselves. But they need help.

I didn't sleep very well that night and I knew why. I was faced with an old question I have asked myself many times—*Why me, here, with so much? . . . And not there, with so little?*

I really don't know the answer, but I know God has His—and somehow we all will have a part to play in its working out. Perhaps my job is to do what I can to make things more fair, more right, here where I am. No—somehow I feel it's more than that . . . perhaps I must look for a way to help my brothers and sisters all over the world, and especially where there is the greatest, most urgent need. Perhaps, when my country is asked to help, to love constructively, to offer something out of its own being to those who lack so many things that we take for granted, I can be one of the many voices which will answer, "What can I do for you today?" . . . and mean it!

Before I can really be effective, however, I must be exposed to the kind of need I don't come across in my daily life. And I can find it here in my own country, even in my own city, as well as in other parts of the world. We have our *have-nots*, too . . . we have our ghettos, we have our hungry children and undernourished adults, we have our illiterates . . . but these aren't the people I see every day. And unless I get to know them, unless I make them part of my life, I won't really understand how urgent their needs are. It's not enough for me to read about them . . . I must *feel* these things, so that they become *my* needs, too. Then I'll be able to do something constructive about them.

We know a young family in our congregation who have been living in the inner city since they were married. In their own quiet way, they wanted to be exposed, too—and we so admired their conviction. They don't believe in being "limousine liberals" who advise from afar but never mingle with the poor. . . . They believe—and are proving—that the *haves* and the *have-nots* can work together to improve both their lives. And they have discovered some wonderful advantages to living in the inner city.

Practically, the cost of living is lower. . . . Real estate is cheaper; they don't need two cars because they can walk to everything; the downtown stores are larger and have more items; they spend more time with their three little boys and less time commuting; they take their children to museums, plays, and lectures more often.

Culturally, they are receiving an education they couldn't get in any school. . . . Their boys go to public school with children who speak nine other languages. . . . They have many different types of neighbors, with different interests and problems, and they are learning to look at all people as individuals rather than as types—"He isn't a color, he's a boy," says young Douglas. . . . They understand now—and they didn't before—that the truly poor aren't always looking for a handout . . . they want to be able to pay their own way . . . they want a chance.

Spiritually, this family has become aware that social action and good intentions alone aren't enough. . . . "Christ *is* the answer, and He is not just a white man's God . . . or a rich man's God. He is *every* man's . . . and we've found that the poor very often know that God is where it's at. . . ."

Dear Lord, let me be here for something. . . .

As I think about the constructive nature of God's love, I can't help imagining what a wonderful influence this characteristic could have on our national and international life. It would be exciting to speculate about what "love lived out" could mean . . . but it could also become a cop-out for me if it kept me from looking to my own life, to my family, to my close relationships. I have to be honest with myself. . . . Am I being constructive where it really counts?

Several years ago I came across the title of a lecture (which I never got to attend) that fascinated me. It was called, "When Is Help Helpful?" and that's what I have to ask myself now. Are there times when my help is not helpful? . . . Am I possibly being destructive rather than constructive?

By helping our children too much we can be destructive to them. We can prevent their developing into the persons God meant them to be. Help becomes a handicap if it is offered in this way.

Sometimes my own children have had to remind me that they don't really need the kind of help I'm offering them. With four children so close together in their ages . . . and all of them being little children together, I got in the habit of giving them little verbal memos . . . "Now, don't forget to say, 'Thank you.' "— "Don't forget to do this or that." Well, the habit was hard to break, but one day as I was reminding our son Tim to thank someone, he said, "Mom, you don't have to say things like that anymore. It's actually worse when you do that than if I forgot to say, 'Thank you.' " Ouch! He was right . . . and I've been trying to remember not to remind my children of things they can very well remember—or forget. They don't need that kind of help anymore.

We can offer help with a pure motive, but if the help isn't really needed, it isn't really helpful. On the other hand, sometimes we may offer help that is needed—but our motives may not be so pure. I'm sure we all can think of times when someone needed help and got it, but the giver then tried to manipulate the life of the receiver. . . . We parents have to be particularly careful here. "After all I've done for you, you're going to leave me?" Sound familiar?

I know of a father who has done countless so-called helpful things for his daughter . . . things that go far beyond the raising and educating of a child . . . things such as setting her up in business, providing her with a fine home, sending her on expensive trips. These may be the things most parents would love to do for their children if they were able . . . things that in themselves are beautiful if there are no strings attached. But they can be destructive if a parent does them as part of the after-all-I've-done-for-you game. And that's what this father has done. How sad it is to see a woman of forty who has never been free to pursue the dreams God has put in her heart because she suffers from a deep sense of guilt and a confused idea of what it means to honor her father. How sad it is to see her constantly in her father's company, with few friends of her own.

I wonder if we honor anyone by allowing him to do something that is destructive to us . . . and to him. And I wonder if the after-all-I've-done-for-you love is love at all. Surely it isn't God's love.

God's love senses when help is really needed . . . and when it's better not to help. He can tell us when our children are able to do things for themselves. . . . He can make us sensitive to their moods. Sometimes it isn't a good idea to offer a helping hand if a child can take care of matters by himself . . . that's when you help him best by respecting his abilities. But if a child's problem is big, and if he really seems to need you, then it's time to do something constructive for him.

As I sit here musing on constructive love . . . as I toss the thoughts around in my own mind . . . I can't help but take a hard look at my own life. And when I do, I have to admit that there are times when my help isn't helpful to the one I want to help most. I tend to be a bit preachy, a bit too eager to find a lesson in anything that goes wrong. But when someone's down, that isn't the time to give him a lecture. I know if I'm in a jam . . . if my time got away from me because I was on the phone too long, and twenty people are coming for dinner in two hours, I don't need a lecture. I need help. Later, when I'm calmer and the last guest has left, I can learn something from my mistakes . . . but not in the midst of them! Well, often I forget that . . . Miss Fix-it takes over and tries to point out to Louie what he did to get in a bind. And when he calls me on it, it hurts. That's only natural, because if we really love our husbands, there is that terrible temptation to try to be the perfect wife—whatever that is.

But then I realize that God is teaching me—through my husband's honesty—how to be more constructive in my loving. And both he (Louie) and He (God) are telling me that I don't have to be perfect for them to love me . . . . and I'm *so* glad! Now, that's *really* constructive love!

Dear God, thank You that You don't keep score . . . or grade us on our performance. Your love is free—but not easy— in my life. Your love is always at work—constructively—in me . . . helping me grow, change, become. As Your love is for me, so may my love be for others. Amen.

4

This love . . . is not possessive . . . .

Free To Be

There was a time when I felt I owned myself . . . that was when I was a very young do-it-yourselfer, trying to earn my way to God by doing all the right things. When some friends told me that this wasn't necessary—that God had done something for me I couldn't do for myself—I said, "Well, what about that verse in the Bible which says, 'God helps those who help themselves'?" To my amazement I learned that there isn't any such verse in the Bible.

I believed in a vague sort of "God out there," but I wasn't yet convinced that I should allow Him to take over. "After all," I thought, "shouldn't I be doing something? Shouldn't I be running at least *part* of the show?"

And then I went on a retreat in the mountains with some of my friends, and one night I couldn't get to sleep. So I got up and took a long walk. But I wasn't alone . . . I felt God was very close, and I said, "Okay, Lord—if I can't earn my way to You, then I just give up. I'm going to find out if my friends are right. I'm going to give myself to You—and to Your Son, Jesus—but You'll have to prove Yourself to me." And at that moment I felt a wave of love come over me. I realized, for the first time, that God loved me for myself—not for what I would or could or should or ought to do for Him. . . . All those

*should*s and *ought*s were out of the way. I was a special person—
because God loved me! That was the most wonderful feeling I
have ever known, and it has never really left me.

As I came back to camp it was time for breakfast and lots
of people were up. And somehow—they looked different to me
. . . they were absolutely beautiful! I loved them—not only my
particular friends, or those who were "my kind of people,"
but all of them. What I didn't know at the time was that the
Holy Spirit was at work in me, filling me with God's *agape*
love . . . and it simply overflowed. I was floating in a sea of
love for all humanity. I was no longer alone or on my own . . .
and I belonged to everyone I saw.

And so much love was coming back to me. . . . I could
actually feel the waves of love washing over me as I walked
along, giving and receiving, giving and receiving. Not a word
was spoken, yet so much was communicated.

Just as my relationship with Jesus changed, so did my other
relationships. I used to feel that I had to work at my friendships . . . giving my friends little gifts and getting together
with them regularly so that they wouldn't think I was neglecting
them. Now I felt that I could be loved and accepted for myself
rather than for what I did. Oh, not that I ignored my friends—
I still did things for them and with them . . . but I did them
because I loved them and not because I felt I had to earn
their love. There's a big difference.

Love is not possessive. . . . What, exactly, does that mean to
me? Not to me, the wife, or me, the mother, but to the very
me . . . the me of me, the person created by God in His image,
the person who has voluntarily chosen to find a new life with
Christ? What does *love is not possessive* mean to me at the core
of my being?

Does it mean that I don't possess my own life? If I have
given it to Christ, do I no longer own it? Yes, that's right . . .
and this is where the journey toward *agape* love really begins.
This love is not possessive—especially with itself. It is not like
human love which sometimes holds back, which often fears that
it will lose everything it gives. God's *agape* love gives everything
away—constantly—with never a thought of getting anything in

return. And yet, so much comes back to the giver . . . for it is through giving and not possessing that we receive.

For instance, when we give ourselves to God—which means that we give Him our love and trust Him to lead us in whatever ways are best for us—we receive His love. . . . And this changes our lives. God loves us unconditionally, with no strings attached, and this is something human love can never do. And so, when we feel accepted, respected, *loved*—just the way we are—we begin to look at ourselves, and at others, differently. Being loved, we want to love . . . having received so much, we're eager to give . . . and the very act of giving fills us with an unbelievable joy. In fact, God's love frees us to discover and grow into the persons we were meant to be. . . . And that's how we find ourselves—through giving ourselves away.

This is what Paul was telling the Corinthians, and it's important for us to understand it, too. The members of the Corinthian church could be pretty mixed-up people . . . they had a lot of hang-ups in their relationships with each other . . . and instead of working together, they sometimes wasted their energies in bickering, competing, and complaining. They were holding onto their own lives, afraid to give them away because they thought they would have nothing left. . . . But Paul was telling them that God's love could free them of their possessiveness. . . . He was reminding them—and us—that God is our great Example. . . . He loved us so much that He gave us Jesus, His only Son.

Sometimes this verse is translated, "Love is not jealous.". . . And when you think about it, jealousy is certainly a form of possessiveness . . . it means that we aren't satisfied with what we have, and we want what belongs to someone else. Not one of us has escaped the nasty clutch of jealousy at some time in our lives . . . and how it can botch up our relationships!

Undoubtedly, all people are equal in the sight of God—but we have to admit that from our human point of view there seems to be some inequality among us. Some of us seem to have supergifts and some seem to have nothing at all. Actually, this isn't true. . . . I believe that while some people may be super-gifted, each one of us has specific talents. While all of us are members of one body, we all can't be eyes, or hands, or lips, or ears. Some of us may even be elbows, and that's fine, because elbows are very much needed!

The Corinthians were just like us . . . . they wanted to use their gifts to serve God, but they were jealous over the way God had distributed gifts among them. And so they held back their abilities . . . possessively . . . instead of letting them benefit each other.

Here is where God's love can make the difference. When we know that God accepts us, we begin to accept ourselves. . . . We stop holding ourselves back, and gradually our talents and abilities begin to emerge because we feel that they are wanted. As our love for others draws us into their lives, as we become part of them, we want to do things for them . . . we want to give them part of ourselves . . . and our individual abilities provide the channel through which we do our giving.

It doesn't matter how many gifts we have, as long as we discover what our particular gifts are . . . and use them. One way to do this is to try ourselves out . . . and let the response of others tell us whether we are doing the right thing. For instance, if we think we want to teach a Sunday-school class, we ought to try doing it . . . and if only two students show up after the first few weeks, then teaching obviously isn't for us. But that's good . . . we found that out, and now we can try something else until we get a better response.

I have always admired people who can go to a meeting and deal with the problems of the present at the same time that they plan ahead for the future. Now, whoever thinks of administration as a gift from God? But it is. I know it isn't *my* gift . . . you wouldn't believe the way I shy away from business meetings. And I know mine isn't the gift of speaking, because even though I do it on rare occasions I don't enjoy it . . . and God wants us to enjoy what we do. No . . . a long time ago I discovered that my talents lie in an area most people don't recognize as a gift at all. . . . I keep getting little nudges to do things— simple things like bringing something to someone . . . a cake, a card, a book, a letter . . . almost anything. This is the gift of helps . . . and it gets me into some unusual situations.

One evening, while I was mopping the kitchen floor, I got one of these little messages telling me to take a copy of Catherine Marshall's book, *A Man Called Peter,* to a young woman in our town. I couldn't imagine why Connie might want or need that particular book so urgently, but there it was—that spiritual poke in the ribs that just won't stop until you say yes. I said yes, but I also said, "Please Lord, not right now . . . I'll do it first thing in the morning." And the next morning I sent the book to her by way of a friend who was going into town and would be driving right by the shop where Connie worked.

That night we had a house full of committee members when the phone rang. It was Connie's husband, Neal, and he was very upset. "Why did you send that book to Connie?" he asked me. It wasn't very easy to explain, but I did the best I could. "I just got a feeling that she needed it," I said. "I don't know why, but it seemed important."

"It was," he said, "and we have to talk to you about it. We're coming over."

"Our house is filled with people," I told him. "It'll be hard to find a place to talk."

"We don't care. We're coming."

When Connie and Neal arrived, I could see that both of them had been crying and I felt their pain. I took them to our bedroom, which offered the only privacy in the house at the moment. And this is the story they shared. . . .

The night before—at the time I was mopping the floor—Neal came home from a trip and found Connie with another man. She had never done anything like that before, and she wasn't quite sure why she did it then. But she was lonely . . . she missed her husband, who traveled a lot . . . and a good-looking young man who worked in a nearby shop asked her to have dinner with him. And one thing led to another . . . which is when Neal arrived home a day earlier than expected.

Hurt, bitter, angry, Neal told Connie he wanted a divorce— immediately. He said he would see a lawyer and talk to her about it the next evening. Connie loved Neal very much . . . and she was as shocked as he was at what she had done . . . but she felt she had no right to plead with him to stay with her. The next morning, sleepless and filled with a terrible guilt, Connie went to work because she couldn't stand being alone with her thoughts. And that's when my friend dropped in and left her a book.

"I remembered you mentioned *A Man Called Peter* once and said it was very good . . . but I couldn't imagine why you suddenly sent it to me at that particular moment. But I took it home with me that night and left it on the coffee table."

Later, as she and Neal sat down to discuss the arrangements for their separation, Neal reached out and picked up the book, nervously turning it over and over in his hands, not really seeing what it was. Then he opened it at a random page—to a sermon by Peter Marshall based on the story of the woman taken in adultery. And he began to read. He read the whole sermon, and then he read it aloud to Connie. It was a message on forgiveness.

"I realized how much pain Connie was going through—and how much I loved her," Neal said. "I had to share the blame for what happened . . . I left her alone too much."

He reached for Connie's hand. "I don't know how to say this, because this has never happened to us before . . . but God came into our lives last night."

By that time all three of us were teary-eyed . . . and I was so grateful for that poke in the ribs while I was mopping the floor.

Years have gone by since that night of forgiveness and new beginnings when God walked into their lives . . . and these very special people have gone on to grow and build a marriage that has strength and fidelity as well as tender love. During these years—often remembering Connie and Neal—I have tried not to question and to be more sensitive to these nudges from (I believe) the Holy Spirit. I wish I could report 100 percent obedience—of course, I can't. Yet, when I *do* move out . . . when I feel somebody needs something . . . however mystifying that something might be . . . there is often (but not always) a warm human adventure at the other end. It's a little gift . . . but I like it!

Love lets us into other people's lives, but *love is not possessive with persons*. . . . There is such a great difference between possessing a person and belonging to him . . . it's the difference between a stranglehold and an embrace . . . between taking over a life and sharing it. And just as we lose our chance to find ourselves when we're possessive with our own lives, we lose those we love when we try to hold onto them. We can be part of those we love only when we free them—help them—to be themselves.

A lot of loving goes on in a family, and it's important for that love to be exchanged freely. . . . That doesn't mean, though, that we should be so unpossessive that we don't even have a feeling of belonging to each other. It means that we should love each other without dominating each other.

God's love builds us up . . . it helps us to develop and grow . . . and that's what can happen in a family if we allow His love to work in our lives. Instead of a husband and wife hanging onto each other, afraid to let each other out of their sight for fear of losing each other, they can encourage each other to develop interests and accomplishments of their own. Instead of parents holding a child close to them when he really is ready to make a life of his own, they can help to prepare him to become part of the world.

Two friends of ours who married a bit late in life seemed to have a sparkling relationship—at least on the surface. There certainly was no lack of signs that they were in love with each other. . . . Joe built a large, beautiful house for Diane and they spent a lot of time together fixing it up. They went everywhere together and did everything together. Often, during the day when Diane was at home alone, the doorbell would ring and a delivery boy would bring her a corsage or a bouquet of flowers commemorating the day they met, or their first date, or one of a hundred little special moments in their lives. They were very conscientious about sending each other birthday cards and anniversary cards, and always bought each other expensive gifts.

Before her marriage Diane had been quite successful as a commercial artist, but Joe didn't want her to continue her career because it would have meant that occasionally she had to travel. Diane understood, and she accepted only those jobs that she could do at home . . . and she seemed satisfied.

Neither Joe nor Diane wanted children . . . at first they simply wanted time to be together, but then they decided that children would take too much of the attention they gave to each other. They used to laugh when we told them how much happiness our children brought to us. . . . "Oh, sure," they'd say, "that's okay for you—but not for us." However, as the years passed, Diane began to long for motherhood, but Joe still said, "What do we want with children? We have each other!"

Eventually, they didn't have each other, because they held on too hard. Diane began to accept some jobs that were especially interesting, even though they involved some traveling, and Joe was miserable until she came home. He complained about her career and tried to talk her out of it until finally she took more and more out-of-town assignments just to get away from his nagging. Joe followed her with frequent telephone calls and dozens of bouquets until Diane began to feel that she was on a string that Joe was pulling too tight.

This "beautiful" marriage came to a bitter end when Diane decided that she couldn't have a life of her own with her husband. Some of their friends were amazed when they separated, but when they began to think about it, they could understand the reasons. Both Diane and Joe—and particularly Joe—had loved each other too possessively. The very thing they feared—losing each other—happened because they tried to hold each other too close.

If only they could have discovered what our friends, the Browns, know . . . that when a husband and wife are secure in each other's love, they can free each other to grow and to care for the needs of others. Shirley Brown is an administrator for a large vital church in California, but that's just one of the many things she does so well. She's a warm, compassionate, trusted counselor for people of all ages, and she's also a successful wife and mother of two lovely, well-adjusted daughters. Grover, her husband, is a busy engineer whose job doesn't end at 5 P.M. He travels a lot, but his marriage has first priority on his time. He is delighted with Shirley's achievements and applauds her efforts to improve herself by taking as many UCLA counseling courses as she can possibly squeeze into her life. In fact, Grover attends most of these courses with her. This couple may forget to send birthday cards, and sometimes they may skip a present, but you can feel the warmth of their love for each other when you're in their presence. No amount of "love signs" could describe their happiness the way their good vibrations do. . . . They are two wonderfully happy people whose love has freed them to grow. And these special people—very special friends— have one of the healthiest, most unpossessive, yet truly together marriages I've known.

It would be fine if all couples could be like the Browns . . .

but today there is an alternative to marriage for those who don't feel the way *they* do about a married relationship. No longer does a man or a woman have to feel that he or she must get married to be accepted in our society . . . and in some instances it's much better for the persons if they don't. This is one of the good developments that has come out of the Women's Movement—and it benefits both sexes. If a person doesn't want to give himself away in marriage . . . or if he feels that he will lose his independence by accepting the love that someone else wants to give to him, that's okay. Then, too, many people are single because they feel called to give themselves to a task that they honestly feel marriage would hinder. Certainly the New Testament confirms this alternative when it speaks of being a eunuch for Jesus' or the Gospel's sake (*see* Matthew 19:12 KJV). I love marriage—but I chose it! And that's the point—marriage is a choice. No one *has to* get married any-more. . . . Single people can build worthwhile lives, too.

The same is true of parenthood, now that we have the means—and the need—to limit the size of our families. Those who think that they would have to sacrifice too much to children or that their energies and time are to be invested elsewhere, needn't have children at all . . . and perhaps it's better this way. Some of the saddest families are those who never wanted to be families . . . the guilt-ridden mothers and fathers who try to hide the fact that they resent their children, and the unwanted children who sense their parents' real feelings no matter how they try to cover them up.

Recently our son Dan said something that touched me deeply. Louie was away for a few days, and Dan, Jim, Andie, and I were compensating by having dinner out. In between bites of a cheeseburger, Dan said, "You know, you and Dad really used to have your hands full with the four of us when we were little . . . and Dad is hard on himself now when he thinks he got really uptight once in a while—but we always felt that we brought you joy." It was hard for me to swallow, and it wasn't the hamburger's fault. "Oh, Dan," I said, "that's so true . . . and it still is! You bring us so much joy!" I could remember my husband through the years, swinging his arms wide and wrapping them around himself as if he were embracing the entire world . . . "Oh, Coke," he'd say, "I just love our kids so *much!*" And I think children sense that. They know whether they're a nuisance or a joy.

Now, for the first time in history, both marriage and parent-hood are a matter of choice . . . and that's good. Because children have a right to parents once they are born . . . and it isn't fair for them to be pushed aside because they weren't wanted in the first place.

Being a parent means giving yourself not only unselfishly, but unpossessively, and here is where many of us have to be careful. If we love our children, it's hard to let them go . . . but go they must when they are ready.

Lately I have been going through a time of reflection—and mourning. I am looking back over twenty busy, happy, some-times hectic years of family life. They were the cocoon years . . . there was the coziness and security of just being together, the six of us . . . warm, close, each one needed within the circle.

The memories are sweet, achingly tender . . . and when I indulge myself in them—as I have been doing—I "puddle up" easily. Not because I am sad . . . but because I am shamelessly sentimental about my family . . . and because I am, quite honestly, mourning the passing of a season, a time I have known and loved. But with three of our four children away at college, it is a season I must now put aside. Often these days I have to remind myself that *love is not possessive* . . . and I ask God to lead me into my next season, which I know will be good and full of exciting adventures if I do not resist it.

But . . . did we *ever* possess our children anyway? When they were small and dependent, did we own them then? No, never. Kahlil Gibran said it, in *The Prophet,* much better than I can.

On Children

> Your children are not your children. . . .
> You are the bows from which your children
> as living arrows are sent forth. . . .
> Let your bending in the archer's hand be
> for gladness;
> For even as He loves the arrow that flies,
> so He loves also the bow that is stable.

We love them . . . care for them . . . train them in God's way . . . give to them . . . and then to complete the love, we must give them away. Love's final act is liberation.

Thank You, Lord, for loving middle-aged parents as well as beautiful young people. . . . Thank You for that love . . . and may it make of me—at this season of my life—the "bow that is stable."

Love is not possessive . . . with things. It's true that when I usually think of possessive love, I think of it in terms of human relationships. Yet many of us value *things* more than anyone in the world.

Some of us hold onto our jobs too tightly . . . we're afraid to let go of our duties for fear that someone else will take the job away from us . . . or worse than that, we compromise our values and do something we know to be wrong, just to hold onto our job.

We all have known young men and women who allowed their ambition to lead them into acts that were criminal and corrupt . . . and what is ambition but a possessive love of power, money, status, position? But there have been other examples, too. . . . We all have also known someone who, when asked to do something that he felt was wrong in order to keep his job, he resigned. . . . He didn't love his job or his title or his status so much that he couldn't let go. Because he didn't possess these things, he was a free man.

And this is what Paul is telling us in this verse. . . . *Love is not possessive with things.* When we have God's *agape* love in us, we don't need anything else. . . . We already have everything. But sometimes we have to lose the things in our life before we realize how much God's love means to us.

I'm remembering what happened years ago in Bel Air, California, when God used a crisis—even a tragedy—to rearrange human values. Louie and I were just finishing breakfast one beautiful morning when we looked out over the valley and saw a puff of smoke rising from one side. We didn't think anything of it, but it was to become the worst brush fire in the area's history. It included numerous fire storms whipped up by the wind into a wall of flames that swept through the hills and canyons—devouring dry trees and brush and much more. Three days later, 465 families were left homeless.

How vividly I can remember the night after the fire when the church families gathered . . . the hall was piled high with blankets, towels, pillows, clothing, food, and all sorts of emergency gear for the burned-out families in the community. We sang, we prayed . . . we made a circle around the families who had lost their homes—and in many cases much more—and then one of us spoke. . . . He was the one many of us thought of as our Apostle Paul, and he said, "Three years ago I was born free through my spiritual birth. This week I have been born free of material possessions." He was Leonard Picker, a man well known in the motion picture industry, both as a film producer and as an executive with United Artists Corporation, and he had come to our church with his wife, Marilee, a few years earlier. They were newlyweds then . . . she was a lovely, young, talented actress with a glowing faith she wanted to share with her new husband, but Leonard, born and brought up in the Jewish tradition, made it quite clear to Louie that he had no intention of becoming a Christian. He came to church because he loved his wife, and that was all!

Fine . . . no one pushed . . . everyone loved . . . and gradually this dynamic man opened up his life to Christ . . . and an apostle was born in our midst. And from the moment he said *yes,* and yielded that powerful personality to God, his life shouted to all of us, "Look! It works! It *really* works!"

And then the fire came. . . .

Marilee was recalling the disaster, too, and recently she wrote to me about it. . . .

Before I tell you what the loss of the house meant to us, I must first tell you a little about the house and how we came to be there.

I had always loved that home, for my folks built it when I was still in high school. Since Mother was an architectural designer and Dad a building contractor, you can imagine the hours of creativity and care that went into the construction.

When my father died, my mother decided to move to Texas. Leonard liked the house, too, so we bought it and moved in just a year before the fire. The loss of my father was still enormously painful and I enjoyed the house not only for its attractiveness, but much more because of the happy memories that were associated with it.

The day of the fire I was at home with my mother, who was visiting from Dallas, and my two daughters—Gina, three and one-half, and Tammy, not quite a year old. We heard that there was a fire and turned on the television to find out where it was. Our house seemed far away from the danger area, but I walked up the hill, thinking I might be able to see the flames. Dark smoke filled the sky, but it seemed so far away. Cars were filing slowly down the mountain past our house—cars filled with people who had just seen their homes burn or had left when the firemen told them to evacuate. I asked several families if they wanted me to take care of their children while they found places to stay—but, fortunately for them, they refused.

We kept watching the news reports on television and I kept watch out the front of our house. I could see the smoke, feel the whirling power of the wind that was blowing the fire away from our house—or so I thought. It was quite by accident that I opened the draperies at the back of our house and saw the other fire looming like a wall of flames on the next hillside, being blown straight toward our house by that tremendous wind.

I told my mother to take the children to her car and leave—she didn't even have time to get a bottle for the baby. I stood, frantically wondering what to take. I put the dog in my car first and then returned to our house, thinking that I would have time to get some things out before I left. I remember standing paralyzed in the living room, wondering what the most important things were. I ran for the photo albums and grabbed the baby books with the children's pictures in them. There wasn't time for more. I ran out of the house into that swirling wind and joined the line of cars that were creeping down the mountainside away from the fire.

There was no way to call Leonard. Only a short time before, when he called me, I had told him not to bother to come home, for we were out of the danger area. In spite of that, Leonard did come home. He ran all the way up that hill, for the police were blocking the cars and trying to keep anyone from entering the area. But only moments after he got within sight of the house, it exploded from the intensity of the heat. Thank God, he saw that the cars were gone and knew that we were not inside the house.

That night when the fire was under control in our part of Bel Air, Leonard and I went back to the house. He had told me that the house was gone, but I was not at all prepared for what I saw. The entire area looked like a bombed-out city. Houses were crumpled into mounds of rubble, chimneys stood like gravestones over the ashes. The streets were buckled from the heat.

As we were driving up the hill I kept thinking that something could be salvaged—after all, *everything* couldn't have been destroyed. I kept thinking of my mother's things—all her heirlooms, packed carefully in metal trunks and stored in one of the rooms—surely they would be safe.

My mind traced the memories of the things we treasured the most. Leonard's books were so special to him, but there was no hope that any of them would have survived—except his Bible, which was in the car at the time. There was the magnificent rose quartz carving that his father had brought back from the Orient many years before. Not only was it a valuable work of art, but, more important, it was very meaningful to both of us because it was from his father who died when Leonard was in college.

I thought of the collection of Dresden and Meissen that had been in my family for generations, and the silver that had belonged to my parents, and some that my grandmother had bought for me in Europe. The gold wedding band that my great-grandfather had made with his own hands for his bride; the sculpture that had been made of our children; the paintings we had collected as we traveled; and there were two pieces of jewelry that I particularly loved—a pearl and ruby bracelet that Leonard's mother gave me as an engagement present and a tiny gold football with a diamond in it that my dad had won in school and had given to me when I was a little girl. It was less than two years since my father's death and I still felt the intense sorrow of that loss. The gold football was my most treasured tangible expression of my memories of him. It was on a charm bracelet and it was the only thing that I really prayed to find as we drove up the hill that night.

We stood in the street, staring at the place where, hours before, our home had been. The ground was hot and burned my feet through the leather soles of my shoes. There was no way that we could walk on the area where the house had been. The entire house had re-formed into a crustation of ashes and stone. Leonard held me while I cried. He was so comforting and his perspective was so different from mine. I could only focus on all that we had lost—he could only focus on the miracle of the lives that had been saved.

When the ashes cooled we went again to the house to see if anything could be salvaged from the rubble. Friends helped us and for hours we worked, trying to find something that was not destroyed. The only thing that remained standing was the fireplace, the metal furniture in the garden and our daughter's metal swing set—the chains hanging loosely where the seats had been. The rose quartz carving was faded to the color of dirty crystal, totally distorted out of shape. The family silver had melted and fused with steel pipes. My mother's metal trunks had melted and everything in them was destroyed. Only two things were removed intact from the debris: a Dresden chocolate cup, the most delicate of china, had been blown by the explosion from its shelf in the kitchen across the dining room and landed, unbroken, on the far side of the living room. The color was bleached out from the fire, leaving only a faint gray pattern where the pink flowers had once been. I still treasure it and keep t as a memento from my great-grandmother. The other item was found as we sifted the ashes in the area where my jewelry had been. There, black from the flames, but restorable, was the charm bracelet holding the gold football that I had prayed for. Also on that charm bracelet was a gold heart that Leonard gave me, which was to have special significance not long after that day.

What unbelievable statistic would there have been that I would find that tiny item out of an entire houseful of broken glass, crumpled walls and rooftop? If I had been asking for a sign of God's comfort and response to prayer, it could not have been more tangibly given.

I want to tell you about Leonard's reaction to the loss, but it is very difficult to get words around those feelings, for his attitude was so unique. I remember how tender that deep voice of his was when he said, "I have you and the children, and that's all that matters." He stood there, seeing everything that we had in the world destroyed, but he didn't see it as a tragedy. The loss of a person is a tragedy —the loss of things is an opportunity to put our trust in a higher treasure. He helped me to see that the things I thought I owned had actually owned me, for I was grieving for them as if they were loved ones. When I argued that I cried for the sentimental things, the irreplaceable keepsakes, he reminded me that I would always keep those memories inside me where nothing could take them away. The things that we hold with our thoughts are ours to keep forever.

I have known people who have chosen lifestyles that are free from possessions, but Leonard lived in the midst of beautiful and valuable things and yet did not allow them to place a claim on him. He loved beauty and enjoyed it around him, but he was emotionally free from the grip that possessions hold on most of us.

We were never closer than during that short period of time that we were together after the fire. Leonard was constantly supportive and I was beginning to feel the contagious victory of his faith. He refused to grieve for possessions and tried to help me see that God could use the loss of our things to lift us to a new level of growth. He wanted me to be free to see what Christ thought was important.

It was only a few weeks after the fire—on Thanksgiving morning—that I saw the real perspective of values. During the night, with no warning, Leonard died in his sleep.

Suddenly the fire and the loss of our home became a most unimportant incident.

For a long time after Leonard's death, I didn't want to own anything. I rented a small house and used some furniture moved from a mountain cabin we owned in Squaw Valley. Gradually I began to care about a home again, but now the perspective is different.

As the months went by, months dealing with grief and loneliness, and the responsibilities of helping my children in

a time that was so painful for all of us, the real priorities of
living became clear to me. Beautiful things are nice to have
and enjoy, but it is people and love and relationships that
matter. Time has passed now—thirteen years—and many
times I find myself tied to some beautiful thing. When I become aware of it I try to remember a time when the values
were explicitly clear.

Leonard didn't want me to be possessed by things. But
also, I know that he didn't want me to be possessed by the
past, by memories—even by love itself. When the time came
to love again, to marry again, I am sure that Leonard re-
joiced in heaven when I was at last free to reach out to a
new commitment—to give myself without reservation to a
remarkable man, and to build a life where even the past—
the joys and love of it—could not possess me and stand in the
way of happiness.

As I put Marilee's letter down, I am filled with nostalgia. . . .
I think of Leonard and his great unpossessive love . . . and the
influence it had on so many of our lives. But that isn't all . . . I
also feel filled with gratitude for Dr. Al Zdenek, the man to whom
Marilee is now married. He is indeed a "remarkable man" and
has this same kind of love that does not possess . . . is not jealous
of the memory of the past . . . but frees the one he loves. But
that should be another story for another time. . . .

For now I will simply fold the pages and put them in my well-
worn folder marked SPECIAL LETTERS—SAVE . . . and thank God
for our friend, Leonard Picker, whose life was telling us—to the
very end—"Look—it *really* works!"

---

*Dear teaching Holy Spirit, in all of life's relationships teach us
the joy of belonging to one another—without the need to possess
one another. . . . Let us drop the strangleholds to make way for
the voluntary embrace. May our possessions not possess us . . . .
help us to put things in their proper perspective, so that we can
use them for the common good.*

*Free us to live in love . . . where we possess not and will not
be possessed, knowing that "love is sufficient unto love." Amen.*

[Quote is from Kahlil Gibran, *The Prophet.*]

5

This love . . . is neither anxious to impress nor does it cherish inflated ideas of its own importance . . . .

Use It—Don't Flaunt It

We all know someone like him . . . a person who talks too much, and always about himself . . . anxious to win approval, and almost desperate to be "onstage, front and center." Our friend was like that—and he was an entertainer, which meant that he was in the spotlight much of the time. But that wasn't enough for him . . . he wanted everybody's attention, *all* of the time.

He was a dear man in so many ways, but most people found it difficult to be with him for more than a few minutes . . . *talk, talk, talk—I . . . I . . . I*—no one else could squeeze in a word. Years went by—he moved and we lost touch—and then we heard that a wonderful change had come into his life. He had become a Christian . . . and then felt a strong call to enter the ministry.

We didn't see him for a long time, and when we did we were amazed. He was so different . . . quiet, warm . . . and with a disarming gift of being able to listen to others—a man who said nothing unless it needed saying. In fact, we found ourselves wishing he would talk more, because what he had to say was so worth hearing. But he didn't feel that he had to be in the spotlight anymore. He didn't need everyone's attention . . . he had enough from God. He was happy using his gifts rather than flaunting them.

When Paul explains that love is not anxious to impress, he is concerned with a specific situation that existed in the church at Corinth . . . and it exists among us today. God had blessed that congregation with many spiritual gifts . . . prophecy, healing, teaching, speaking in tongues and more . . . but some of the members were inordinately proud of their particular abilities. Apparently, they talked about them and loved to show them off, but they didn't do very much with them. . . . And Paul is reminding the Corinthians that while it is important for people to discover their special gifts, there is no reason for anyone to be impressed with them. Pride, Paul says, is not compatible with God's kind of love.

By no means was Paul putting down spiritual gifts. In the previous chapter and the one following 1 Corinthians 13, he urges the Corinthians to use their gifts. But here he is warning against their misuse. Enjoy what you do well, he is saying, but don't become obsessed with it. . . . Use your gift . . . don't flaunt it.

How very much we need this advice! For the church is being given these spiritual gifts today . . . and we need to be reminded that they are God's gifts, not ours. We are to use them in the body—the church—and they are for our edification, yes, but mainly for the benefit of our brothers and sisters . . . which is why they were given to us in the first place.

I have witnessed the practical ministry that spiritual gifts can bring to a life . . . and to a congregation. It began years ago in a church we were serving . . . and I will never forget what a beautiful experience it was to watch people opening up like flowers to receive from God. The gifts were bona fide—there was no doubt in my mind about that. But I would be less than honest if I did not say that with the new life and enthusiasm the Holy Spirit was generating in our fellowship, there were also potential problems. Some who did not have certain gifts were feeling left out—even judged and pressured by a few others who felt that everyone should have his own gift.

Early in these developments Louie and Ted, our much-loved associate minister, jumped in with both feet . . . they believed fully in spiritual gifts, but did not believe that one gift should be made the talisman of the Holy Spirit in a life. They counseled and taught in depth on the diversity of gifts . . . the importance of not having superior or inferior feelings relating to the gifts . . . the necessity for all God's people to yield themselves to *Him,* to receive whatever gifts *He* wants them to have—and to use. The result was a beautiful spirit of openness that moved among our people—and a very real work of the Holy Spirit in our midst which was validated by a new caring and personal ministry . . . and love—oh!—such love.

President Emeritus Dr. John MacKay of Princeton Theological Seminary has written in an article for *World Vision* magazine:

> What is known as the charismatic movement—a movement marked by spiritual enthusiasm and special gifts, and which crosses all boundaries of culture, race, age, and church tradition, is profoundly significant. A product of the Holy Spirit . . . it is marked by a passionate love of Jesus Christ and the dedication of time and talent to His service among people everywhere. . . .

We experienced this personal "love of Jesus Christ and the dedication of time and talent to His service," and within a short time we found that we had a corps of lay ministers within our church . . . people who could be called upon to pray for the ill, or to sit up all night with an alcoholic who was trying not to take a drink, or to comfort someone in mourning. As the gifts were shared generously throughout the congregation, no one felt left out anymore. We all were grateful for the love and life they brought to our church. And so it has been through the years—and is now . . . our ministries have been blessed (and I mean blessed!) by lay people who became ministers in the true sense—through the work of God's Holy Spirit in their lives.

Some people feel threatened by the gifts of the Spirit, believing that they bring trouble to a church—as they did to the Corinthian congregation . . . but they don't have to, not if we do not "major" in the gifts—but in their *Giver* . . . not if we allow God's love to teach us how to use them . . . and not if we remember whose gifts they really are.

In an earlier chapter (1 Corinthians 3:3) and in one that follows (2 Corinthians 12:20), Paul discusses another problem in the church . . . one that certainly is related to pride. He warns against disorders in the meetings and at the Lord's Table, implying that some Christians were pretty uppity about their social status . . . humiliating the poor and unfortunate, and making them feel unwelcome.

One of the most painful things for me, personally, to see is a spirit of exclusivism take over a church. It reminds me of an ad for a retirement home which read, "Exclusive, gracious living in a truly Christian atmosphere." But if we truly follow Christ, then we can't be exclusive . . . because the church is made up of all of us . . . not just some of us who feel comfortable with each other.

Some years ago a young woman who joined the congregation we were then serving showed us that we needed her even more than she needed us. She came from a very deprived background, and had hesitated for a long time about coming to our services because she thought she would be out of place. Finally she overcame her reluctance and one Sunday there she was. . . . She was overdressed for the occasion. . . . She had bought a new black dress that was very fancy and, unknown to her, the price tag was still hanging down from one of the sleeves. She wore a great big hat . . . and she was very noticeable in a congregation that was strictly casual. I loved her the moment I saw the fear and anticipation in her large brown eyes . . . I knew how much it meant to her to worship in a church again.

Later a friend of mine told me that a woman standing next to her noticed our visitor immediately, and definitely not with approval. She asked my friend who she was, and when my friend informed her, she sniffed and said, "Well, my dear, why would she want to join *our* church? What could she possibly have in common with *us?*"

My friend answered, "How about Jesus? Isn't He the One we all have in common?"

(And I say, "Here! Here!")

Fortunately the attitude of exclusivism didn't prevail in that church, and our visitor became a very loved member who taught us a valuable lesson. She awakened in us a broadness of mind, a willingness to accept people who were a little different from most of us. Her very presence taught us that more than education, culture, race—more than anything else—it is Christ who makes us one in the Spirit . . . and without Him there can be no unity in the church.

I have already admitted that I am impatient with people who

are impatient with people, and when I see uppity attitudes prevail in any church I can hardly stand it. I want to shout to the congregation, "Look—all of us—look!—Love isn't . . . *cannot* be boastful, or uppity, or puffed up!" And yet, if I were to do such a thing I would be acting out of my own feelings of love, and not out of God's *agape* love in me. There's a lesson here that I must learn . . . for I am in danger of becoming somewhat uppity myself. I am forgetting what the church really is. . . . It is not a home for saints . . . it's a hospital for sinners! There will always be some members who are impressed with themselves . . . there will always be some who have not yet arrived at the place where they can accept everybody. But they need understanding and love, too—perhaps even more—so they must be made to feel welcome, too. While I cannot accept their attitude, I cannot exclude *them*. I must welcome them and pray that in time they— and I—will be changed by God's love working among us.

As I muse about the practical meaning of **Love does not cherish inflated ideas of its own importance,** I wonder, dear Lord, just how one becomes inflated with one's self. You say that I am to love myself . . . respect myself . . . and love others in the same way. Yet I must not become puffed up, so that I can see nothing but myself. Yes . . . I think I understand now. You are speaking about a balanced attitude. . . . You are pointing out the difference between a healthy appreciation and an unhealthy obsession with the self. . . . Great God of Balance, show me where to draw the line. . . .

I wonder if You mean that a person who is filled with God's love simply doesn't take himself too seriously. Perhaps You're telling us that we should learn to laugh at ourselves.

A friend of mine, the wife of a singer, understood that. . . . I remember the day I walked into her kitchen many years ago and found her standing at the sink with her hands in dishwater, chuckling softly to herself.

"Okay," I said, "what's so funny?"

"Something that happened at the concert last night," she said. "I was sitting behind two women who didn't know I was there. And when my husband came onstage one of the women leaned over and whispered to the other, 'Isn't he marvelous!' [And her husband is—and was—a very handsome man.] Then the other woman leaned over and whispered, 'And his wife is nice, too, in a very *plain* sort of way.' "

Now my friend is far from plain—she's lovely—but she just doesn't take herself seriously. And I think it's a delightful characteristic.

I wonder, too, if the person who can laugh at himself can also accept his imperfections. He knows he's going to make some mistakes in life, and when he does, he doesn't overreact to them. He doesn't agonize for hours over a silly goof, or play the if-only-I-hadn't game. And that reminds me of today. . . .

Today I made a mistake—a silly, senseless, dumb, goofy mistake. It didn't hurt anyone but me and my pride. But I've been kicking myself ever since, until just a moment ago.

When I told my husband what I had done . . . and what a "doofus" of a wife he has, instead of being impatient or gaping at me in dismay and disbelief—he laughed. It helped when he laughed. It made me feel good . . . made me take myself less seriously. And finally it made me laugh, too. Love—God's love in our lives—will keep us from becoming puffed up. Could it be that this same love will encourage a sense of humor in our lives?

Vain, frightened, insecure people find it hard to laugh at themselves . . . but God's love keeps us from becoming vain, and it gives us a sense of inner security in Him, freeing us to humor and laughter. Someone (sorry *Someone,* I can't remember your name) said, "Laughter is from the intelligence of the heart." . . . And someone else (this time I do remember . . . it was Hugh Sidey of *Time* magazine) said, "Laughter is a bridge to communication and understanding."

What a practical, everyday gift love brings when it keeps us from being vain . . . and from taking ourselves too seriously. God wants us to learn from our mistakes, not to stand in judgment of ourselves when we do something wrong. God's love doesn't flog itself . . . it forgives.

I've always noticed that when we're hard on ourselves, we're hard on other people . . . and when we expect a lot from ourselves we expect a lot from others. And so it goes, all the way down the line. Yet the person who expects too much is seldom happy. . . . Ironically, because he expects too much, he can never be satisfied. He misses out on all the joy he might find in himself and in other people because he sets up a barrier of expectations between himself and others—and between himself and Jesus. Until Jesus breaks down this barrier, God's love can't work in him . . . and that might take a long time.

My daughter Andie summed it up very well when I asked her, "What does it mean to you when a person is inflated with his own importance?" And she said, "Well, he'd be so full of himself, there wouldn't be much room for God."

Napoleon must have been that kind of a person . . . because he is quoted as saying, "I am not a man like other men. The laws of morality do not apply to me." In other words, he was saying, "I am above the law," and that attitude can get people in a lot of trouble. When we think we are *that* different, *that* important, we begin stepping on others, and sooner or later they have to show us how vulnerable we really are.

When I think of the people I know who really have good reasons to be proud of their accomplishments, I find that they are also those who do not dwell on themselves. In fact, it's often hard to get them to talk about themselves at all . . . not out of false modesty, but because they are so interested in other things and other people.

Sometimes we take not only ourselves but our causes too seriously . . . and that can also lead us into trouble. Recently a woman tried to convince me that it was time for our country to stop worrying about the poor and underprivileged . . . because, as she put it, "We middle classers are the underprivileged now." She was complaining about high prices, high taxes, and the strain they were making on her family's standard of living—which, incidentally, was quite good. Her words disturbed me . . . but I was even more disturbed when I began to read similar words in newspaper articles quoting some of our government officials who were concerned about the growing need for food in some of the little nations in our world. "You've got to look out for Number One," seemed to be the theme of it all. For years we have given to other nations out of our abundance, but now that abundance is dwindling. We must decide whether we will share our daily bread. . . . The outcome will depend upon whether we act out of human love . . . or God's love.

Human love has its limits . . . it sees the suffering in our world, but it puts Number One first. God's love is so different

. . . it gives out of its everyday supply . . . and strangely, wonderfully, there is always enough.

When I think about people who are puffed up, boastful, proud, attention-grabbing, exclusive, a question comes to my mind. . . . Just how much love is enough? Because it seems to me that a person who is impressed with himself is actually someone who is unsure of himself. He seems to keep trying to get from others what he really needs from God—a sense of inner security. Not that a person "has it made" when he opens up to God's love. . . . There are times in life when we all tremble . . . I do, and so do you. But when God is in us, when His love warms us, then we know that we're important to Him. This gives us our basic security . . . and even when we tremble, we do it in a kind of holy confidence. . . . We trust God to bring us through the rough spots. . . . We take His hand and follow, even if we don't know where He is leading us. Our sureness is not of ourselves . . . we can only be sure of God. And until we learn to rely on Him . . . until we give ourselves over to Him . . . we will always be dependent upon the approval and attention of others. We all need—must have—human love. But no amount of human love will ever be enough. How ironic that this boastfulness, this need to advertise ourselves, this pride comes not from an abundance of God's love, but a scarcity of it.

In a fine little book by Bernard Berkowitz and others, entitled *How to Be Your Own Best Friend,* I came across this portion of a dialogue which offers some insight into people who feel they must call attention to themselves:

> "There are plenty of people who see nothing but their bright spots, and are always talking about themselves. They think they're quite satisfactory as they are and if anything is wrong, it's with somebody else, not them."

> "Well, of course, but they don't really believe it. Those who are working that hard to convince themselves and others how great they are, are also shutting something out. They can't see their faults because they're afraid they've got nothing else. They think their choice is between being perfect and being the worst thing that ever lived. The trouble is it's very hard to give up that way of looking at yourself, because

it's based on refusing to look into yourself. And to change, you really must look into yourself to see what you're doing wrong. You must be able to see the ways you're putting yourself down, and just decide that isn't what you want to do. Then you can start doing the things that give you pride and pleasure of living."

While boasters may be hard to take, we can't turn our backs on them, for it is through us that God's love may be working its way toward them. They need our understanding rather than our judgment . . . and they need our honesty. For if we love them enough we will be able to tell them that they talk too much. Of course, that means that boasters will have to stop talking long enough to listen . . . and sometimes they don't. Ah, yes, but when we can't find a way to speak the truth in love, God can . . . as long as we keep trying.

A teacher friend of ours was faced with a problem when his elderly predecessor—a man who was retiring—was breaking him into his new job. The older man was an endless talker who spoke of nothing but himself. Our poor friend was at the end of his patience and was about to tell the man that he could do very well without him, thank you, when he began to pray for guidance. And suddenly he seemed to see beneath the surface of the old man . . . he saw that his nonstop chatter was a plea for love, for a little recognition that he had accomplished something during his life. He simply wanted another human being to say, "Yes, you've done very well. . . . I can see that." So our friend did say it . . . patiently, kindly, and in a spirit of *agape* love. He began to listen to the old man, to ask him questions about his life. . . . He affirmed that he had been a dedicated teacher, a loving husband, and a fine father. Then gradually the boasting stopped, the talker began to listen and take an interest in things other than himself . . . and our friend made a most enjoyable new friend.

The Scriptures are like diamonds . . . with so many different facets of light. From the Greek fathers comes another facet of light on the phrase: *Love does not cherish inflated ideas of its own importance.* To the early Greeks this meant that a person who is filled with God's love will not hesitate to perform the most menial tasks, or to endure scoffs as he goes about his humble service. What a wonderful example our Lord has set for us!

Love is not above doing the lowly—even the dirty—job . . . because love is not anxious to impress. Love wants to serve. . . . Love does not have to play the hero roles.

When our phone rang one evening the call was from a close friend and member of our church. My heart sank as I heard the desperation in his voice and words. His son, a sensitive, intelligent, sixteen-year-old boy for whom the problems of the world had become too great had just shot himself and was near death in the hospital. Minutes later, my husband came home and immediately left for the hospital to be with the family. He was by the boy's side when he died later that night.

It's an agonizing time for a family . . . with papers to sign and arrangements to be made . . . and while our friends—the boy's mother and father—endured the business aspects of death at the hospital, my husband turned to the boy's older brother and said, "Let's go back to your house and see what we can do there." Louie imagined what it would be like for them to come home to a bloodstained room—and to him the logical thing to do was clean it up before they returned.

It was a humble thing they did . . . cleaning the blood from the walls . . . cutting away the blood-soaked carpet and replacing it with a remnant they found in the garage . . . restoring the house to the way it was before the tragedy so that the father and mother could begin to remember what had been, instead of what had been destroyed. It was love serving in the best way it could . . . and it seemed a little thing to Louie. So little, in fact, that he never mentioned it to me. But many weeks later the boy's father told me that although he had always loved Louie, and respected him as a preacher and leader, nothing Louie had ever done—in or out of the pulpit—had touched him as much personally as that simple act of service and love on the night of their tragedy. Then he told me what had taken place . . . a small thing, a witness to the truth of what the ancient Greek fathers once said . . . that love performs menial tasks simply because it *does love.*

Perhaps, too, Paul meant that love—God's love—will not step on others to get its own way. . . . Yes . . . this love is not inconsiderate. . . . For when we are inconsiderate we really are saying, *"I'm* the important one—not you" . . . and God never puts Himself first.

When we are filled with His love, we are realistic about our own needs and considerate of the needs of others. . . . Realistic and considerate—these are two very practical commodities that make us more complete as human beings. Ah, yes . . . now I can see how love is indeed an everyday thing!

But, you know, we are programmed to develop inflated ideas of our own importance. Our society tells us that if we don't take care of Number One, no one else will. . . . Our magazine ads tell us we "deserve the very best," and everything around us seems to work against a humble, realistic view of our own importance. How, then, can we attain it?

This morning we woke up to a pleasant surprise. During the night it had snowed, and when we looked out the window—there it was—instant beauty!

Whenever I wake up to this silent, white fairyland, I want to keep my husband and children home and go out and throw snowballs . . . and sometimes it works out that way when the roads become impassable. But usually I have to accept the fact that snow time can't always be playtime, and so this morning I dutifully drove the car pool to school, and reluctantly watched Louie leave for church. Then I got to work—picking up after the youth-group dinner the night before and finally settling down in my favorite "writing rocker"—paper and pen in hand.

The hours have flown by as I have been thinking, praying, and writing. . . . Just now I got up to peek out the window at my winter wonderland—and could hardly believe my eyes. The snow —except for little dabs here and there on the lawn—was completely gone. The sun had warmed our earth and melted almost every trace of the cold night.

How very much this reminds me of the Sun of my soul . . . and the way His love melts away old habits that have plagued me. Of course, I must take responsibility . . . I must be "response-able"—but the real miracle in me is the warmth of His love, working from the inside out. His love does for us what we can never do for ourselves . . . it deprograms us . . . not in a day, as the sun melts the snow, but just as surely. I feel as if I am "in process," for during all the years since I gave my life to Jesus, He has been working in me, on me . . . sometimes through me . . . melting away the frozen areas of my life, revealing new areas, new attitudes, new possibilities that have never been used.

Nothing brings me back to earth faster than the door opening and banging closed . . . announcing the arrival of my two still-at-home children. Jim runs upstairs (all fifteen years and six feet one inch of him) and sits on the edge of the bed as I write.

"Jim, what do you think it means to have an inflated idea of your own importance?" I ask.

"H-m-m." Silence. "H-m-m." Silence again. "It would be like looking at yourself through a magnifying glass—and at everyone else through the wrong end of a telescope."

Now, I wonder why I didn't ask him in the first place. . . .

Remind me, dear Lord, whose person I am . . . whose capabilities these are that I use each day of my life. . . . Keep my ego slim—healthy, yes, but never puffed up. . . . Let the needs of others be in the foreground of my vision. . . . Give me an insight into my own feelings so that I can feel with others. . . . Keep me from becoming vain—and that even means that I must not exaggerate or dwell on my errors. Sometimes I need perspective, Lord . . . and that means the gift of laughter. . . . And when I achieve, I want to remember who makes it possible and thank You with all my heart. Amen.

6

This love . . . has good manners . . . .

Breeding Will Tell

It was an absolutely gorgeous night . . . the sky clear, the stars twinkly, the air crisp and slightly chilly. As we entered the elegant lobby of our host's apartment building, we were surrounded with another kind of beauty—man-made, but almost as lovely. I found myself looking forward, more than usual, to the dinner party. . . . I was accompanying my husband on a speaking trip, and it was a nice break in our schedule.

We took the elevator up to the penthouse and stepped out into one of the most perfectly appointed homes I have ever seen . . . the tables, the flowers, the china and silver and crystal, the music were beautiful . . . each one in its proper place and chosen with perfect taste. And the people! . . . They looked beautiful, too, in black tie and long gowns . . . so graceful and well mannered. As I think back to that night, I can still see the receiving line— a pageant of color and beauty—and I remember feeling an eagerness to get to know some of the people in this elegant parade.

A little later we sat down to dinner—Louie and I at different tables—and the food, like everything else, was superb . . . carefully selected, meticulously prepared. It was like a dream—until the dinner-table conversation began. And then, I found it hard to believe what I was hearing—for out of the mouths of these "beautiful people" came—well, some of the most morally obscene talk I have ever heard. . . . Not that the language was profane —these people knew better than to use such words socially—but their conversation seemed totally lacking in human kindness.

Deftly, wittily, they put down every group that wasn't their own—nationalities, young people, races, political groups—and then they went on to dissect specific individuals who didn't conform to their way of thinking. They slipped the knife in so graciously and turned it so skillfully. Their cruel jokes belittled everyone or everything they didn't like, and the more cutting the remark, the more vigorous the laughter (although they were too well bred to laugh very loud). I'm still amazed that so many people who seemed to feel the same way about *everything* would be together at one time and in one place. Finally they chose as their target a person I knew quite well . . . and at that point my feelings would no longer let me be silent. I put my fork down and said, "Excuse me . . . I'm sorry, but I have to say something. . . . I just can't agree with our conversation at this table." I went on to tell them my views—which probably sounded just as dogmatic to them as theirs did to me—but at least they were different. Well, I'm afraid I spoiled the evening for the other guests at my table. First I was met with silence . . . and then, as the conversation staggered to a wobbly start, each person prefaced his remarks with, "If you'll excuse me for saying this, Mrs. Evans. . . ." It was pretty bad.

I thought the party would never end. Later, as my husband I were going down in the elevator, he asked, "How was it at your table?"

"Well," I said, "that was a pretty elegant party—on the outside. But I had trouble with the inside attitudes."

"It was the same at my table," he said. "I just had to speak up."

"Me, too!"

For days afterward I felt sick whenever I thought about that night. But I had to think about it because there was a lesson in it for me . . . one I wanted very much to understand. Only when I remembered Paul saying: *Love has good manners,* did I realize that the party was an example of manners gone wrong. The guests knew and followed all the rules of social etiquette, to be sure, but love and simple human kindness had been lost along the way. And proper manners that exist only on the surface of our lives have nothing to do with God's kind of love-manners.

I really don't know how manners ever got started in this world, but I assume that originally they must have been intended to meet a need . . . such as pulling out a chair for someone who was about to sit down or holding a door open. It's not as if we can't do these things for ourselves . . . but it's especially nice when someone does them for us. Yes, it's true . . . good manners meet a person's inner need to be kind . . . they are the thoughtful gestures that come from a heart motivated by love. To RSVP is a thoughtful thing to do because you let someone know you are coming and they can prepare for your arrival . . . writing a thank-you note is a kind thing to do—besides, it feels good to express gratitude. Shaking hands is kind . . . and it puts us in contact with the other person.

When we are filled with God's love, we sense the human need for a touch of love even before it becomes apparent . . . and we respond. . . . Our behavior toward others is motivated by His love, not by protocol . . . we are kindly rather than correct . . . and not only toward those we feel are "our people," but toward everyone.

Manners are something we use—or should use—every day. They aren't just for dinner parties or other social events. Recently a friend of mine took a taxi to the railroad terminal and as the driver dodged in and out of the busy city traffic he said, "You know why there are more accidents these days? It's because people aren't driving courteously, the way they used to." So manners can become a matter of life and death.

When Paul writes: *Love has good manners,* he is describing our life-style as Christians. While the old saying, "Manners make the man," may be stretching a point, the manner in which we treat others does reveal something about the inner quality of our lives. . . . And if God is our Father, this is the best breeding we can possibly have. If His love is in us, if it fills us to the point where it spills over, then our manners will be genuine . . . they will come from the heart. Even when we are under pressure—as we all are these days—even when we are troubled with the economic, moral, and political problems of our nation, even when we must wait on long lines to get some of the things we need, or when there aren't enough check-out counters open at the supermarket, or when something in our personal lives is not going well, we will not be rude, uptight or cranky with others

. . . especially with those who serve us. Of course, there are
times for all of us when God's love is *not* having its way in us
. . . and we *are* cranky and rude. But we will not want to be—
nor will we try to justify being that way . . . rather, without
flogging ourselves, we go on, knowing that there is "a more excellent way."

As Christians, we aren't bound to a book of etiquette, but we
do need an example . . . someone who has both inner and outer
breeding . . . and we have One in Jesus. There were standards
of acceptable behavior in His day—just as there are in ours—but
there were times when He didn't live by them. Jesus did what He
felt was right . . . He acted out of love . . . and sometimes that
meant that He cut across the cultural standards of His day. Think
of the way He behaved toward the woman who sat at His feet
and washed them with her tears . . . or the woman taken in
adultery . . . or the Samaritan woman at the well. If He had
done the socially accepted thing, He wouldn't have had anything
to do with those women . . . He wouldn't even have been seen
with any of them. They were outcasts, considered sources of
uncleanness . . . the kind of people one would never invite to
dinner, ill-bred persons who burst into private little get-togethers
and spoke to strangers without a proper introduction. There
were others, too—the tax collector, the leper, the beggar, and all
the little, forgotten people of the world. Manners, to Jesus, were
not meaningless rituals . . . they were the way in which He
reacted to people—all people. His behavior was governed not by
propriety, but by God's *agape* love for man.

Sometimes I feel that the socially accepted way of doing things
can be cold, even unkind. . . . And I wonder whether our
Christian life-style shouldn't be put before our cultural traditions.

Love has good manners. . . . When Paul wrote these words he
was probably referring not only to the personal lives of the people
in the Corinthian church, but also to the way they worshiped
together. We know that the Spirit of God was at work in that
group, with the gifts of the Spirit very much in evidence. We also
know that when the power of Pentecost is present, it is sometimes
difficult for people to contain the expression of that new affection.
Probably there were disturbances at their meetings, interruptions,
unmannerly behavior, rudeness—all of it prompted by impatience

and a tremendous zeal to serve God. But, in such a charged atmosphere, some people were bound to be hurt, and so Paul reminded the Corinthians that God's *agape* love—which was the source of their new experience—had another dimension. . . . "[Love] doth not behave itself unseemly" (KJV) . . . "It is not arrogant or rude" (RSV).

Here is where we seem to be quite different from the Corinthians of the early church. They had an abundance of enthusiasm, while some of us don't seem to have enough. Our problem is not that we interrupt each other, but that many of us don't respond at all. One of our much-loved professors said, "I can understand the atheist—and the person on fire for Christ—but for the life of me, I can't understand the lukewarm Christian!" Many of our congregations are so well mannered in the cultural, socially accepted sense, that it's difficult for a genuine spontaneous burst of love and praise to God to find a place in our worship. As Christians, we may need to loosen up a bit and go in a Corinthian direction . . . it's a matter of letting our faith express itself. One of Daddy Evans's favorite sayings is, "Impression without expression means *de*pression." And something as great and powerful as the love of God *needs* to be expressed. The love of God among joyous Christians is a warm, exhilarating experience each one of us is meant to know.

As with all these other love characteristics, the best place to begin putting good manners into practice is right at home. And yet home is so often the place where we are loved the most and behave the worst.

Kindness at home means observing simple courtesies that create an atmosphere of respect for the differences and opinions of others. No fair talking love—and walking all over the members of our family in inconsiderate actions. No fair talking love—and treating those we love the most with disrespect.

I had a phone call a few days ago from a mother who was concerned about her teen-aged son . . . and I am troubled even now by what she said. She assured me again and again that it was her great love for him that made her worry so. . . . He was going with a girl of whom she didn't approve, and from the letters he got from the girl, his mother suspected that he was not behaving in a trustworthy way. When I asked her how she knew what the letters contained, she said she had steamed them open without her son's knowledge.

It seems to me that the way to teach trust within a family is not by opening another person's mail . . . for if we invade each other's privacy at one point, we will probably do it in other areas as well. To put it plainly, that's bad manners—any way you look at it! It may be the kind of thing we would do out of human love (though I even doubt that) but it's not what God's love would ever prompt us to do.

When we are motivated by God's *agape* love we become much bigger persons. We don't feel challenged or insecure because some members of our family are different from us. We respect their uniqueness . . . we allow them to do things their way . . . because the love in a family should be great enough to cover these differences among individuals. This is the way God our own Father loves us, His children.

Instead of putting down our children with critical remarks about the things they like, we can look for something appealing in their music or in the way they dress. We may not like the *dum-dum, dum-dum* of their songs, but perhaps if we listen to the lyrics we'll find them good . . . and we ought to say so.

There are so many ways in which our manners—the way we treat others—can become a powerful influence in our children's lives. So it's important to pay attention to what we say and do. Are we encouraging them to use and develop their judgment? If my daughter and I are shopping and she exudes over something she thinks is great . . . do I say, "Oh, you like *that?*" . . . in that certain tone of voice that really says, "I think your judgment is terrible"? Or do I say, "Well, I'm glad you like it," and try to see what it is that appeals to her?

One of the quickest ways to cut off communication with our children is to be rude to their friends . . . and we do this whenever we disapprove of them. When we say something like, "Ooh, how can you go out with them again" we're really saying, "I don't trust you, and I don't respect your feelings." It's true that sometimes we may worry about the kind of friends our children choose and we have the right to be honest with them about our concerns —but we can also learn something . . . because they choose them for a reason. There's something in those friends that our children perceive and like . . . and we should try to discover what it is so that we can appreciate it, too. That's acting out of love—and it's using the best of manners.

The same is true about the way we treat our husbands and wives. If we are reflecting God's love in us, we'll respect our partner's right to be an individual. We won't always interrupt him when he talks . . . and—worse than that—we won't do all the talking *for* him.

Some time ago, in one of our small study groups made up of several married couples, a husband and wife had fallen into a habit that was noticeable to everyone but them. Whenever Ben, the husband, opened his mouth to say something, Lydia, his wife, cut him off by telling us what he meant to say. If Ben managed to say a few words before Lydia interrupted, she restated his words, beginning with, "What Ben really wants to say is. . . ." One night Steve, another member of the group, could take it no longer. He asked Ben a question and when Lydia began to answer, Steve flushed red in the face, banged his heavy fist down on the table and shouted to her, "Stop it! Don't you see what you're doing to him?"

Lydia stopped and looked around at all of us, completely confused. "What?" she asked. "What am I doing?" She had been her husband's interpreter for so long that she wasn't even aware of it. Gently, with a great deal of love, the group began to point out to her that she was attacking her husband's sense of self-worth. Steve was especially helpful . . . for he could speak from experience. His first wife, from whom he was divorced, had done the same thing to him until one day he simply had to get away from her. "It took me a long time to put the pieces of my confidence back together—and when I see you doing the same thing to Ben, I feel as if I'm coming apart again," he said.

Gradually Lydia became aware of the many little ways in which she displayed a lack of respect for her husband. It all began many years ago when she was unable to accept the slow, thoughtful way in which Ben spoke, and so she tried to hurry him up by interrupting and putting words in his mouth. Quite plainly, she was rude, but Ben was too well mannered to object, even though inwardly he smoldered with resentment.

An interesting thing happened when this couple's inner feelings were brought out into the open within the security of a group of loving fellow human beings. Both Ben and Lydia seemed so relieved . . . they became far more open and sensitive to each other. We could actually see God's love beginning to fill the areas that had been occupied by hurt and stubbornness. They took a new delight in each other's special, individual qualities . . . and as their inner love simply spilled over, their manners greatly improved.

How much I need and appreciate the people who speak the truth in love to me. My children and my husband are especially dear to me in this sense (though I may not always think so at the time)—they just don't let me get away with much! Through their loving honesty God makes me grow and stretch. Of course, growing and stretching can be painful at times . . . but whoever promised us *real* life without pain?

I think it was Albert Schweitzer who said, "There is so much loneliness in the world because we are afraid to be as cordial as we really are." How often we experience a warmth of love toward a person—perhaps even a person we don't really know—and yet we keep it inside us. We're afraid to go up to someone on the street and say, "Hello," or "What a wonderful smile you have—I'd like to know you." Don't you ever feel these things? I do. But usually we hang back, thinking that it wouldn't be the mannerly thing to do . . . and how wrong that is! For good manners is a demonstration of our love for another human being, and the world is hungry for such signs of brotherhood.

Just imagine what might happen globally if we as a nation were to express our love for other nations in a visible form—regardless of protocol. How much better it would be to use love's tools instead of the forces of destruction as the ultimate test of what is right and wrong. As Jesus showed us, manners that spring from a heart of love are more potent than the machines of war. . . .

I've been trying to think of the best-mannered person I know, and one particular woman keeps coming to mind. Her name is Mimi, and she is beautiful in every sense of the word. She comes from a family of means who were able to train her in all the social graces, but the most beautiful thing about her is that she is as well bred on the inside as she is on the outside. Her manners are heart-deep and she has a unique way of expressing to others the love she receives from God. She and her husband, George, are gifted with a creative kindness. For instance, for months on end I have watched Mimi and her husband taking meals to a couple who are limited by finances, age, and miserable health. She does this not because these people are related to her or because they are "her kind"—which they aren't—but because she heard of their need and felt nudged by the Holy Spirit to "put them in her basket." And the most marvelous part of her service is that she does it so kindly and quietly . . . she simply helps in whatever way she can and then disappears, acting in the name of the Lord so that the credit goes to Him. Her good manners are so gentle and real that she makes each recipient feel he is doing her a favor by accepting her love.

How much I want to—need to—learn from her!

As I reflect on manners, it seems to me that they change every now and then. Some traditions are dropped from use when they become irrelevant to contemporary life-styles. . . . When they become stodgy reminders of the past, they may even obstruct kindness and real love, and it's good to be rid of them. To be of any value at all, manners and social customs need to serve people . . . and as long as they are relevant to human needs they will be acceptable in any age or era.

I suppose most of us, as children, were taught not to talk to strangers—not only as a safety measure, but as a sign of good manners. And yet that's a bad habit to get into . . . for a person is a stranger only if we make him one. Or, as Helen Steiner Rice expressed it so delightfully in one of her poems, "Strangers are friends we haven't met."

Louie and I had a friend who was the most uninhibited people-meeter we ever knew. His name was Don Hall, and he had friends in all parts of the world because he had the good love-manners to go up to almost anyone and say hello. We used to enjoy traveling with him and his equally warm wife, Millie, because we never felt as if we were among strangers. Whether it was the innkeeper, the driver of the boat, or the man on the street, Don Hall went up and took the person's hand, said hello, and before we knew it they were having a great conversation. It was wonderful to see how people responded to him, too, and through the years after their meeting, Don and his many new friends would keep in touch with each other. Don just wasn't afraid to be as cordial as he really was inside.

These are the kind of manners I wish we could pass on to our children—and to all children everywhere—but admittedly it isn't easy to do. We have to warn our children against getting into cars with strangers—such manners are relevant to our world. But in being anxious to protect them from the very real dangers of our society, we must also pray to find a way to encourage them to be as cordial as they really are.

Our daughter Andie leaves for school early in the morning, and during the winter it is still quite dark when her car pool drops her across the street from the campus. One morning this past winter, as she was crossing the street, she saw someone standing—swaying, really—on the sidewalk outside her school. As she approached the form, she saw the figure of a man . . . his face covered with blood . . . glasses broken. He was an old man, obviously dazed. There was no one else in sight.

Andie remembered what she had been taught as a child . . . also, there had been a special assembly at school where the students were warned against speaking to strangers. . . . A young girl at a nearby campus had been found murdered and the police suspected it was done by someone the girl didn't know.

Andie stopped for a moment and then she thought, "What do I do now? Do I just go on to class and mind my own business, or do I find out what's wrong with this man?" As she hesitated, the man tried to speak, but he was incoherent. Perhaps he had had a stroke, or a fall? There was no way for her to know. So her next question was, "What do I do? What *can* I do?"

In the face of her training her inner feelings told her to stay with the man until help came. And this is what she did. Within a few minutes one of her teachers—a man—came by and was able to get the help that was needed.

When Andie told me about the incident later that day, I could sense that a tug-of-war had gone on inside her. It had been dark, and naturally she was afraid. But somewhere inside her there was enough light to distinguish the difference between danger and human need.

To her it was a simple thing. "I just couldn't leave him, Mom," she told me. "Not until some help came."

She had acted out of love, responding to a need that couldn't be voiced. . . . And I believe she did the right thing. For as we teach our children caution and good sense—and manners—we must also make sure that the cord of human kindness is woven through all their lessons. Or else we're going to live in a separated world.

Perhaps this distinction is one we can't make on our own, for love isn't something we can teach. It is something we must *be*—with God's help. . . . And if there is enough of His love running through our lives, some of it is bound to rub off on others and be seen in our actions . . . and maybe especially in our *reactions*—to others, and to life.

Dear Lord, may my manners—that is, the manner in which I treat others—undergird rather than undercut . . . bolster rather than belittle. Make me more concerned with kindness than with always being correct . . . more concerned with people than with protocol. Ensure all this by making my actions and reactions simply an overflow of Your love in my life. Thank You for Jesus! In His name, Amen.

7

This love . . . does not pursue selfish advantage. It is not touchy . . . .

Tender—But Not Touchy

You can forget to send me a birthday card . . . I'll never notice it. If you don't invite us to your next clambake, I'll think you're being considerate of our busy schedule. If we are walking down the street toward each other . . . and you suddenly cross to the other side . . . I won't think you're trying to ignore me. I'll just know you needed to get to the other side. I can be magnanimous about almost anything and anybody—except my family. That's where I'm vulnerable . . . sensitive—yes, touchy—because that's where I love the most. Be unkind, unfair, unduly critical of my family, and you will have pushed my "touchy button." I am very tender there . . . and what is tender can become touchy. That is how I know, once again, that my love—left to its own—will not be enough for the big or the small things in life. God's *agape* love just has to come to the rescue.

A woman in one of our congregations once invited us to tea so that she could tell us—because she loved us, she said—that people were beginning to talk about the company we were keeping. One particular person—we had a deep friendship with him . . . he was a brother . . . and as I listened to the woman advising us to break off our relationship with him, I felt my blood rising and my touchy button went off. I wanted to stick up for my husband . . . protect him . . . support him—and our friend—

which really meant putting the woman in her place . . . none of which was the right response to the occasion, but I couldn't help it because love *is* touchy.

Well, Louie handled the situation very well . . . . he gently told our advisor that we would continue the friendship and that he was a minister to all the people, not just to some. But I was too upset to keep quiet. "He's our friend!" I exclaimed, still not believing what I had heard, and thinking that somehow that would explain everything.

I couldn't sleep that night because I was just plain angry with the woman. I wanted to ask God to bless her . . . I wanted to be able to say I loved her . . . but I couldn't . . . not yet. Before I went to bed I had prayed, "Lord, help me. . . . I know I've got to get the right attitude about this." And then as I tossed and turned—wrestling it out with myself—I prayed, "Lord, I know I need help. . . . I've got a real problem here—I'm too touchy about things like this—especially about this woman. Give me Your mind." And then I went to sleep.

In the middle of the night I woke up. A lovely peace had come to me . . . my anger was gone, and I knew then that I had come to the place where I could pray, "God bless that woman because she doesn't really know what she's doing . . . and help us to be strong in being able to take this kind of remark and yet live the way we feel You want us to live." What I couldn't do with my own limited supply of love, Jesus had done for me . . . what my own mind couldn't accept—which was that I could love the woman and still disagree with her—the mind of Christ had accepted for me. The woman didn't have to change—I was able to love her and ask God to bless her right where she was—and exactly as she was . . . although I could hope that in time, and in an atmosphere of love, she *would* change. And I assure you I never would have been able to do that on my own.

Paul had already pointed out to the Corinthians that some of them were rude to each other. . . . Now he was speaking to those who were *hurt* by slights, exclusivism, and prejudice, reminding them that they, too, were very much in need of God's *agape* love. **This love is not touchy**, he said . . . meaning that when people are rude to us we are not to respond in kind.

Paul could speak on this subject with authority and from personal experience, for apparently he had a tender spot and could be touchy indeed. But he also knew that love is the best remedy for supersensitivity . . . he was a transformed person.

Most people, given a crisis, cope unusually well. It's the petty annoyances and frustrations that get us down. And so Paul had a message for all of us . . . for everyone is touchy at some point.

But most people seem to have certain times when they are touchier than others—I know I do. There are times when I look at the garage—which ordinarily doesn't bother me at all—and suddenly want my husband and sons to clean it up. I want their tools, their bikes, and their pieces of lumber put away—somewhere, anywhere, as long as the garage looks neat and tidy. And if my husband doesn't tell me he loves me at least ten times each day, then I'm inclined to think he doesn't. This has been going on for twenty years, but my family understands me . . . they know me very well . . . and they respond with the best possible antidote—humor. "Oh-oh, Mom's after the garage again," our sons will say . . . and Louie will glance at the calendar and tell me that in a few days I'll know that he loves me just as much as he always has.

But men have these moments, too . . . so my husband assures me. When business pressures are high, when they are working on important projects, or when they are trying to solve personal or family problems . . . men, too, have their touchy times.

While we cannot change ourselves, Paul says, we can be changed by God, just as he was. . . . A finer, better spirit can take over in our lives if only we will let it happen.

This is true in my own life . . . . for when I walk close to God I am a different person. I feel loving, forgiving, untouchy. . . . But when I am not close to God, when I am seeing things only through my eyes, I become supersensitive . . . that's when my touchy button is likely to go off at the slightest pressure.

The difference, in practical terms, is that we are either God-centered or self-centered, and that determines what we see in life. When God is at the center of our attention, it takes a pretty big obstacle to distract us, and when it does we can deal with it in the security of our knowledge that God loves us. We aren't under the pressure to be perfect . . . we can make mistakes . . . and we don't have to be loved by everybody (nice as that would be!). On the other hand, when our lives are centered on ourselves, there is very little room for God. We don't have the calmness that comes from feeling loved by Him, and so we are easily upset, threatened, and frustrated by all the petty things in life. Not having enough inner love for ourselves, we seek it from others and cannot stand the pain if we are rejected. And so, to avoid being hurt, we ward off love itself. . . . We become prickly.

The prickliest person I've ever known was a very attractive, intelligent, and remarkably talented man . . . just the kind of person who ought to have a lot of friends and a busy life. But it didn't work that way for him. . . . He was a lonely person who projected on everyone the dislike he had for himself. He was so touchy that he turned away every offer of friendship, every gesture of love, with a remark such as, "Oh, you don't really want to do that for me," or a look that asked, "What's in it for you?" Many people poured themselves out to him, each one thinking, "I'm going to be the one to reach him," but no one succeeded. Underneath his well-groomed exterior was a man starving for the love that only God could give him, and which he wouldn't accept. He was a very "religious" person who believed in God with all his mind—but not with all his heart. And so the most important experience in life had eluded him. . . . God had never become real to him, never become part of him . . . and when he spoke of love, he meant *his* kind of love—human love—and that simply wasn't enough. Never knowing what God's love really meant, he couldn't identify it when he saw it reflected in others.

Nancy, however, was something else. When I first met her, I thought I had never met anyone like her . . . . young, lovely, bright, well educated—and trained to be completely helpless. Yes, Nancy had been brought up to be "a lady," which, in her case, meant that she was dependent on almost everyone for almost everything. "When I got married," she told me, "I couldn't even boil an egg—literally!" Her life revolved around herself—not because she was so fascinated with her own life, but because it was a habit. And, yes, she was a prickly person . . . because all of life was very hard for her—marriage was hard, children were hard, work was hard . . . and no one could give her the kind of help she expected to receive. She took offense easily. She suffered frequently from back problems and all sorts of minor physical ailments which offered her a bit of escape from the constant irritations she felt. She couldn't take criticism, not even the slightest hint of it, and although she said she wanted everyone to love her, what she really wanted was their approval.

Eventually Nancy became worn out by her own touchiness and she realized that she had to do something about the way she lived. Her irritability was affecting not only herself, but her husband and children. So she reached out to the one Person she hadn't asked for help—and she got it. She was very new in her dependence on Jesus, and she had given only a small amount of herself to Him . . . but it was a beginning. The warmth of the love she felt gave her the courage to look at herself honestly . . . and she saw that she was the one who was causing most of the frustrations in her life. Realizing that she had to untangle the knots in her emotions or waste her life in a struggle against them, Nancy took steps to get practical solutions to her problems—first from her minister, then from a psychiatrist who worked in tandem with the minister, and then from the members of her church who gave her the loving support she needed when the going was rough. It was a long time before Nancy felt that she was a self-sufficient human being who could do things for herself, but when it happened it was exciting to watch. Gradually this emotionally fragile, frightened girl became an outgoing, gutsy woman who not only accomplished brilliantly, but accomplished what few people believed could be done. Instead of thinking that life owed her something, she looked for ways in which she could give herself to life. . . . She was a source of practical inspiration in her own church and in other churches as well, as she shared her honest pilgrimage with other strugglers. As she continued to grow, she discovered and used talents she never knew she had . . . and she isn't afraid to put them on the line. She knows that God loves her . . . and that has healed the sore, tender areas of her being. She has become one of the least touchy persons I know.

There are some trees that are more flexible, more able to bend, than others . . . and it seems to me that people who have the Spirit of God in them are like those trees. They don't break under pressure . . . they aren't destroyed by strong winds . . . they yield to them in the assurance that when the wind passes they will be able to stand straight and tall again.

Or you could say that untouchy people are able to bounce back. . . . They're like marvelous little corks that simply can't be held down by the heavy tides and waves in life. They feel things, they

get hurt sometimes—but they can absorb the pain as well as they
can the joy of life—and *pop!* they're back on the surface of things,
bobbing along. Yes, love—God's love—has this delightful ability
to bounce back.

There is a Greek word, *malakian,* which means "soft-skinned."
It describes certain sea creatures of "soft substance, without a
protecting, external shell." This is the word used for "infirmity"
in the Greek translation of Matthew 10:1 RSV: "And he . . . gave
them [his disciples] authority over unclean spirits, to cast them
out, and to heal every disease and every *infirmity*" (italics mine).

Many of us have this kind of infirmity, this soft-skinned condition. . . . We are so easily bruised by life. That's why this verse
in Matthew is such good news for us. It means that we don't have
to carry this burden around anymore . . . we don't have to become involved in the silly, unnecessary problems that arise because we are supersensitive. We can be cured of our infirmity
. . . healed! God has this power, not only over physical diseases,
but emotional ills as well . . . . and He *wants* to heal us.

In his First Letter to the Corinthians Paul isn't telling us to
become insensitive when he warns us about our touchiness . . .
he's not saying that we won't be hurt by what we see and feel in
life. No . . . the more we love, the more we will be hurt . . .
but if it is God's love that we are expressing, then we won't have
to stay hurt. . . . We won't bruise, because God's *agape* love has
this great healing power. When someone does something that
prompts a touchy response in us, we can take the hurt to Jesus—
immediately—and lay it at His feet. I know it works, because I've
done it. . . . I've also refused to do it at times, savoring my
sensitivity and pain, allowing myself to wallow in touchiness,
watching the afflicted area turn black and blue and remain sore
for weeks. And even then I'm not free of it . . . no matter how
hard I struggle to forgive the person who hurt me, my mind keeps
going back to the hurt itself, and somehow the pain gets worse,
not better. It's too much for me . . . and finally I have to pray,
"Help me, Father, because I just can't do this myself. . . . I know
You love this person, and I need Your help to love him, too. . . ."
That's when something begins to happen. Once I allow God's
agape love to have its way in me, it acts as a great circulatory
system, drawing out all the soreness and discoloration in the

bruised areas of my being. Soon I'm whole again . . . . yes, I know it works.

One Sunday morning, many years back, when our daughter Andie was about two years old, we were hurrying to get ready for church and Louie noticed Andie sitting on the floor in the living room trying to put on her shoes and socks. She was a strong-willed little gal (as were all our children, and we loved it!), and while it was good for her to try to do things for herself, she was having a terrible struggle with her *ga-ga's,* which is what she called her shoes and socks. There just didn't seem to be time to let her continue, so Louie knelt down by her and said, "Here, Andie, let me do it."

"No! No!" she said, "Andie put on ga-ga's!"

"Honey, we're in a hurry," Louie said. "Let me do it." He put on the little socks, peeled them over, put her feet in her shoes and tied the laces. "There," he said, and left the room.

A few minutes later we found Andie still in the middle of the living-room floor with her shoes and socks off. She was trying unsuccessfully to put them on again. "Andie do it," she said determinedly. . . . "Andie put on ga-ga's!" . . . Then the frustration became too great and she began to cry. She looked up at Louie and said, "Daddy, help—put Andie's ga-ga's on." And so a bit of maturity was added to a two-year-old when she learned to let go . . . and let someone else do something for her that, at that point, she could not do for herself.

That's exactly how we all behave at times. We're like strong-willed little children who insist on doing things our own way until we find that we can't handle some situations without God's help. As we mature, as we allow God's love to motivate us, we give in more easily . . . we want our own way less and less often. We see that His way is much better.

Jesus was the supreme example of this openness. In Gethsemane when He prayed, "Let the cup pass from me . . . nevertheless, not my will, but Yours," He wanted a way other than the cross, but He didn't insist on it. (*See* Matthew 26:39.) And through His willingness to let God the Father have His way, we all have been blessed beyond words.

When we're touchy . . . when we're self-centered rather than God-centered . . . we're more likely to insist on our own way in life. We have our rights, yes . . . but so does God, and it's a matter of which ones we put first. If we concentrate on our own rights, if we're so touchy that we must have everything our way, we may be blind to the gifts and talents that God has in mind for us. . . . We may never arrive at the place where God wants us to be—and I strongly believe that each of us has a place in this world where we can achieve our greatest potential as human beings . . . and for God. But we can't find the way by ourselves, for sometimes it takes odd little twists and unexpected turns—we need God to get there.

Sometimes it takes a little honesty and criticism to get us going in the right direction—but I must admit that some criticism is hard to take. It's especially difficult if we're soft-skinned, because usually we put so much stake in our own plans that we can't accept anyone else's ideas. And yet, someone else may have a better way. . . .

Criticism is a touchy subject in itself. . . . When someone comes up to me and says, ever so sweetly, "It's because I really love you that I'm going to tell you this," my guard goes up. Honesty in the name of love can be cruel, and perhaps this is why most of us—myself included—have trouble accepting some criticism . . . the kind that isn't given in love—at least not in God's *agape* love.

How different it is in a small *covenant* group I have been in for some time. . . . These women are truly my sisters and I can accept their criticism—in fact, even seek it—because they have already given me their love. We have been together so long in this matrix of God-motivated love that we have earned the right to mirror back to each other some things that we could not see for ourselves and really want to change. But even more than that, I know that my sisters are going to stand with me as I look into myself . . . they will help me to change . . . they will affirm my progress every step of the way. . . . And all the while I know that they love me—even when the changes are slow. Now that's the kind of loving feedback and constructive criticism I like!

I think that the same loving matrix has to be established before we can go to others. We really don't have the right to go up to someone and tell him how we think he could become a better person—that isn't speaking the truth in love, and it usually can't be received that way. On a national level, it's something else . . .

we have to speak out strongly on important issues and principles, but that isn't the same as criticizing a person on a one-to-one level. When it comes to that, we have to earn the right to speak the truth by creating an aura of love in which our words will nurture rather than wound.

We also have to be willing to stand by the person who wants to accept our ideas and feelings. This is a very vulnerable time in a friend's life, and we are needed in many ways . . . to encourage him to take a step in a new direction . . . to help him get up when he stumbles, and to share in his joy as he becomes what he wants to be. In a very real sense, we become a partner in making the change, once a person is aware that a change is desirable. And when we are willing to do this, we won't have to tell a friend that we love him before we speak the truth. . . . He'll feel it.

Love is not touchy . . . but it can be—and ought to be—*angry,* at times. Often the two responses are lumped together, and they shouldn't be, for they are not the same. Jesus was able to express His anger, and so should we, for anger and love both spring from the same capacity for deep feelings. . . . If we really love people . . . if God's *agape* love is working in our lives . . . then we're going to see things that arouse our anger. If someone is harming my child, my love is going to rear up and say, "You can't do that to my child!" . . . and that anger is part of my love. For some reason, many people feel it is okay to be prickly and irritable, but never angry. . . . Yet in the life of Jesus we see the opposite. Angry? Yes, at times. But touchy and self-centered? Never!

Perhaps if we deal honestly and quickly with our anger, we will be less sensitive and touchy about the things that disturb us. This is particularly important in a marriage, where the Scripture, ". . . do not let the sun go down on your anger" (Ephesians 4:26 RSV) is most relevant. Human love, as we have seen, is tender and sensitive, and in any marriage worth its salt, there are bound to be misunderstandings and disagreements . . . but if those hurt feelings and that anger aren't brought out into the open, they'll go deeper and deeper, festering until they infect the whole relationship. If we let things go until the next day . . . if we allow ourselves to cool down . . . that may be too late. The next morning you wake up (that is, if you got any sleep at all) with things to do . . . children are leaving for school, a husband has to get to work, and so you carry your anger for another whole day. There may be demands on your time that evening, and so another sun sets before you find time to talk. Days may pass before there's a break in your busy schedule, and by then there is a barrier between you.

It happens to all couples . . . it has happened to us . . . these differences, these misunderstandings . . . and many times we have walked the beaches—or the parks or the city streets—late at night and even into the next sunrise, because we knew that we had to make things right between us. That coming back together has to take priority over everything, no matter what else has to wait its turn. Neither of us is able to function well with that terrible wrenching feeling deep inside that comes when we misunderstand each other . . . it's like being pulled apart physically, which of course it is in every other sense. And so, we do without some sleep, and the next day we're pretty tired, but our peace has been won. . . . We understand each other again, and so it's okay. There is that wonderful feeling of healing and wholeness inside and we don't mind being sleepy.

Yes, anger is something we all have to deal with . . . but first we have to distinguish it from irritability. In speaking about touchiness, Paul is not referring to temperament or disposition . . . . some of us have shorter fuses than others, but Paul makes it clear that we can't use our temperament as an excuse to be touchy. He knew that supersensitivity could ruin relationships, wreck homes with sarcasm and sullenness, and nullify true fellowship with the community of believers. And so he pleads with the Corinthians to let Christ indwell their hearts with His love. We don't have to struggle on our own with our limited resources . . . we can be shaped by a love that has far greater power. And we don't have to wonder whether we're angry or irritable . . . because God's love is *never* touchy!

It is almost five o'clock . . . time for me to begin preparing dinner. Soon my family will be coming home . . . and I know I am carrying a burden I do not want them to share. It's an uneasy feeling that all is not right with me, yet I don't know precisely what happened to make me feel irritable. Nothing big stands out in my mind . . . it was just an ordinary day.

I've had this feeling before, now and then, and I know what I must do. . . . I must give up the little irritations that are getting to me . . . I must give them up to Jesus in sort of an instant yielding and be free of them. No matter how unimportant they seem to be . . . they are making me sour for my family, and they deserve better than that.

I sit down and I pray. . . . All right, Lord, there's something bothering me. . . . I don't even know what it is, so please show it to me and let me take care of it.

And then I remember . . . a telephone call, one of many throughout the day, but this one particularly hard to take because the caller implied some unpleasant things about someone . . . and then there was the young man who came to the door selling magazines. . . . I had all the magazines I needed and I tried to be kind and looked for one I could subscribe to for a year, but he wanted me to sign up for three years and I couldn't . . . so he went away mad and I felt as if I had let him down. . . .

One by one all the funny little things that have accumulated during the day come out into the open where I can see them for what they are. . . . And one by one I give them to Jesus, praying for the persons involved and working out what needs to be done. Now a feeling of peace is coming over me. My mind is getting uncluttered. . . . Things are sorting out. . . . Perhaps one or two problems remain for me to talk over with Louie and Jim and Andie . . . I need their thinking, their objectivity, their feeling for what is best to do. And I know they will give it to me. But I don't have to face them with my mind on some distant thoughts . . . I can give them my attention and listen to what has gone on in their lives today. They, too, may have problems to solve.

Thank You, Lord! I feel so much better. And there's the front door opening now. . . .

Dear Father make me so sure of Your love . . . so secure in my knowledge of it . . . that I may be able to respond to life—and the people in my life—with Your magnanimous love rather than with prickly irritability. I know my love is not enough . . . so let me drink deep from Your well of love—love that is always tender and never touchy. In Jesus' name. Amen.

8

This love . . . does not compile statistics of evil or gloat over the wickedness of other people . . . .

The Good Guys and the Bad Guys

In *What Do You Say After You Say Hello?*, Eric Berne discussed what he called "psychological trading stamps." These are the hurts people collect and cash in when they feel they have justification. Berne wrote:

> Some people go over their hurts and angers every night before going to sleep, others do it less frequently; while still others only do it when they are bored and have nothing better to do. Some wait until they need one big justification, and then count up all their hurts and angers in the hope that they have enough to warrant an outburst of anger, a "free" sulk, or some other dramatic emotional display. Some people like to save them and some like to spend them.

By an odd coincidence, Louie and I had just read this book a few days before we had dinner with Susan and her husband, Keith. We had always sensed that Susan carried some bitterness inside her, but we didn't realize how deep—or how painful—it was until that night when we began talking about Eric Berne's concept of trading stamps. We thought it was extremely interesting and helpful in understanding the reasons behind some of our human problems. So did Susan . . . and she immediately began applying it to her own life.

She went to the desk and brought back a pad and pen, and there at the table she began making a list of the hurts she had collected from her guardian, a woman who had brought her up after her parents died. "Yes," she said eagerly, writing so fast that her words were a scribble, "there's this stamp," and then she would tell us about something her guardian had done to make her angry. "And this—and this—and this. . . ." The list was getting long, and Susan was very angry.

"There!" she said at last, holding the paper at arm's length. "I've got a whole book of trading stamps!"

"What are you going to do with them?" Louie asked.

"I don't know," she said, frowning.

"Would you like to cash them in?" Louie said.

"Yes, oh, yes!" she said. She was near tears and her hands were clenched. Her eyes turned to the fireplace where some logs were burning cozily.

"You can," he said.

Susan hesitated a moment, clearly reluctant to give up her long-stored treasure. Then she spoke again . . . but it was different this time. She was no longer simply reciting grievances . . . she had dropped her guard, let the tears fall, and was allowing us to see the real emotions behind the "statistics of evil" she had been listing. She was angry—yes—but anger was not the primary emotion. Behind it lay hurt, bewilderment, and a feeling that when both parents were taken from her she no longer belonged to anyone. Hurting as she was, it was easy to see how her guardian —well meaning, I'm sure—could do things that hurt and offended her even more.

Finally she nodded her head and stood up. There was a spontaneous clasping of hands as Keith, Louie, and I stood with her and walked across the room toward the fireplace. It was a big decision for Susan to make, and we weren't sure she would go through with it.

She stopped in front of the fire. We all prayed . . . and suddenly Susan dropped the paper into the fire and we watched it burn into a blue-black smudge. There were hugs all around . . . and the expression on Susan's face was beautiful . . . so peaceful, so full of joy. She was free.

It was more than a gesture, for in the weeks that followed, Susan was able to get in touch with her guardian, whom she had not seen for several years, and renewed a relationship with her. Now that she was a grown woman and not a little child, she also found that the woman seemed quite different to her . . . in fact, there were many things about her that Susan really liked! Gradually she was able to emerge from a past that had trapped her into holding a grudge against someone who had hurt her. . . . And this is what Paul is urging all of us to do.

It is just as important for us to get rid of our "stamp books" as it is for those who have committed injustices to learn to love. It makes no sense to hold onto them until we feel we have the right to get even . . . or until some other little slight makes us feel that we are justified in losing our temper. Keeping statistics of evil . . . keeping accounts of all the big and little hurts, insults, and offenses we have experienced . . . is injurious to our health and our sense of well-being. It is also at odds with God's love.

In a sense we can choose our memories—not by repressing the painful ones, but by forgiving them. The Greek word for "keeping statistics of evil" is *logizesthai,* which is an accountant's word for entering an item in a ledger so that it will not be forgotten. So whether we burn our stamp books or tear up our ledgers, the truth is that having faced the hurt . . . having worked it out . . . having forgiven the injuring party, we then can *choose* to dwell on it no more.

Someone said of Abraham Lincoln, "He never forgot a kindness, never remembered a wrong." There are courses in memory retention—but perhaps I need a course in the art of forgetting, for I find that I'm not as good a forgetter as Lincoln. . . . I cannot be sure that a hurtful situation will not at some time be brought back to my mind. But if God's love has been at work in me . . . if I have truly gotten rid of my stored-up angers and forgiven whoever was responsible for them . . . the memory has been defanged. When it makes its appearance, it no longer wounds.

If love does not gloat over the wickedness of others, then what about our own wickedness? Some people are generous with others, but oh! so hard on themselves. When they goof or are downright evil, they may confess their sins and do whatever can be done to make the situation right with the people they have hurt . . . but they refuse to forgive themselves.

In a study group one of my friends attended, there was a very heavy woman named Ellen who seemed to be trying to eat herself to death. She didn't care how big and fat she got, and when she talked about her weight it was obvious that it was her way of punishing herself for a sin she couldn't forgive. Many years ago she had become pregnant before marrying the man who was the father of her child. Her son was now grown and happy, her husband was well on his way in an exciting career . . . but throughout all that time Ellen had carried a terrible burden of self-condemnation. Finally it was more than she could bear and she clearly wanted to die . . . even though her family tried desperately hard to show her they loved her.

As Ellen opened up more and more to the group, the other members could see that she was a warm, concerned, generous human being, and they reached out to her with their affection. Then she began missing some of the meetings, coming only occasionally. One day, when Ellen showed up after having been absent for two weeks, my friend couldn't help herself. . . . "Ellen," she said, her eyes filling with tears, "Why haven't you been coming to the meetings? I feel hurt by that because I'm concerned about you . . . I love you, and it hurts me when you push my love aside." Later my friend told me, "Honestly, I don't know what came over me—I've never spoken like that to anyone in my life!" But Ellen just stared at her and then at every other member of the group. "I didn't know," she said, "I really didn't know that anyone loved me."

The group thought they had broken through to her . . . but the next week she didn't come back . . . and she never came to any of the meetings again. She refused to speak to any of the women on the phone and simply cut herself off from them. . . . She couldn't believe that she was lovable—and forgivable.

Poor God! . . . What can He do for us when we refuse to believe Him . . . to take Him at His word . . . and to follow His loving example? If He forgives, why shouldn't we forgive? . . . and stop compiling statistics of evil against others *and* ourselves? No one is more miserable than someone who is constantly putting himself down. . . . In our family we call it "rolling in the thorns." How much better to accept our Father's Word . . . and walk free.

And yet it's very hard for us to accept His Word. . . . It isn't something we can handle intellectually . . . it doesn't seem to be logical or rational . . . we can't put it together or take it apart to prove that it works. So many of us seem to have grown past the point where we can simply believe. . . . Simplicity—yes, that's what we need to recapture if we are to take God at His Word when He tells us He will forgive us *anything*. How amazing it is that if we want to mature as Christians, we must become more childlike in our ability to trust.

I know a lovely young girl who was doing the opposite of what Ellen did—but for the same reasons. Lottie was starving herself to death. She was down to eighty-five pounds—just skin and bones—and while she said she just didn't want to get fat, she was plainly self-destructive. She never missed a chance to criticize herself or poke fun at something she had done. . . . "I'm a terrible wife," she'd say . . . "I'm the worst mother my kids could have." And she was completely unaware that in belittling God's creation—herself—she was also belittling God.

Lottie even saw faults where there weren't any, and that's often the way of the statistics-keeper. . . . She would imagine she had done something wrong when in truth she hadn't, and suddenly she would show up at a friend's house with a gift as an apology for an imagined slight that never happened.

Finally Lottie's friends couldn't take it anymore and they began to point out what she was doing to herself. She was absolutely amazed . . . she knew that she had a low opinion of herself, but she didn't realize it was so obvious—or destructive. Little by little, she began to look into herself and she was frightened by what she saw—a total absence of love for herself. Since childhood she had mouthed the words, "Jesus loves me, this I know," but unlike a little child, she hadn't let the love-feeling get inside her.

Gradually, with the help of friends and some extensive counseling, this girl is opening up to the wonderful fact that God does indeed love her very much. She began with such a tiny amount of faith in that promise, but that was the beginning of a new life. Now her faith is growing and she is learning a whole new way of thinking . . . the process of "becoming" is slow and painful and there are many setbacks . . . but it is working. Whenever she has destructive thoughts about herself, whenever that old accusing voice says, "Boy, are you lousy!" she knows that she must hold on tightly to what she now knows is true— "I'm a child of God . . . God loves me." And from there she can take another step—"My husband loves me . . . my children love me . . . other people love me . . . and I'm not going to put down this creation of God's! *I'm a worthy person!*" Slowly, with great apprehension, Lottie is opening her hands . . . the grudges she held against herself are slipping from her fingers and she is lifting them up to receive the gift—just like a little child.

It's interesting that *love does not compile statistics of evil* comes close behind *love is not touchy*. Perhaps Paul is pointing out to us that when we allow ourselves to be too touchy, we may take the next step and become resentful—which is what keeping these statistics is all about.

What a burden . . . what a bore—keeping all those records. (I dislike bookkeeping, anyway!) And how wonderful that we have been shown a more excellent way—the way of a life dominated by Christ . . . a life secure in God's love so that we are able to share this love with others.

As a woman in one of our study groups said, after describing a personal experience she did not want repeated, "None of you has the need to hold this against me. . . . So I can share it with you, and you can help me with it." Love simply has no need to keep accounts of evil.

When people break down . . . go astray . . . fall flat . . . there is an ugly temptation for most of us to gloat over their failure. It has a strange effect on us, making us feel bad-good, if you know what I mean. . . . We sort of think, "Hm-m-m, that just proves that I'm the good guy and he's the bad guy. . . . I was against him all along, and now he's confirmed the fact that I was right!" Oh, we can just wallow in it!

But that isn't love—not God's love—because God's love *does not gloat over the wickedness of other people*. No rubbing our hands together over a juicy bit of gossip, or enjoying someone else's scandal.

The city of Corinth offered lots of opportunity for both gossip and scandal. It was a swinging city known for its vice . . . and in that setting Paul says, "Love is never glad when others go wrong . . ." (1 Corinthians 13:6 MOFFATT).

People within the church can be particularly vulnerable when it comes to taking a holy pleasure in the mistakes of others. . . . It's such a subtle thing, this pulling ourselves up while pushing someone else down. It can give us a sense of moral superiority which some of us find delicious. But love—*agape* love—takes no delight in scandal even if it is true. It wants to know the truth—yes . . . it wants to take the mantle off the sin that has been committed . . . but love weeps when truth is sad . . . and it looks for ways to help the ones who have fallen.

When I think of love not gloating over wickedness . . . and love able to give up a grudge, I think of our good friend Ralph Hamburger. Ralph was grieved more deeply than almost anyone I have ever known over one of the ugliest truths that has ever been uncovered in this world. . . . When he was a young boy living in Holland, the son of a Lutheran mother and a Jewish father, his country was taken over by the Nazis in the years just before World War II. The persecution he saw sickened him, and in his late teens, during the years 1942 to 1945, he worked with the Dutch underground where his responsibility was to hide Jewish and political refugees before they could be arrested and sent to concentration camps . . . and death. He also helped with the distribution of underground newspapers.

Following the war, he felt strangely drawn to the United States, which is where we met—at the Hollywood Presbyterian Church in 1947. Although he was a confirmed member of the Netherlands Reformed Church, Christ did not become real to him until he came to this country. For many months he struggled with pent-up feelings of hatred and anger toward the German people, but in the end he realized that such feelings were incompatible with his new life in Christ. Hate was giving way to love. It was then he began to share with some of us who met for prayer on Friday nights his dream to take a team of young people to Germany and other parts of Europe to share Christ and to help rebuild the countries which were so devastated by war. His zest, his enormous love, were contagious, and many responded. Louie and I were among those he reached with his message. . . . We were students in those days, not yet married, and we joined the first group of young people who went overseas to work . . . with the support and active cooperation of the Reverend Walt James, who became the father of the Overseas Deputation Work at the Hollywood Presbyterian Church. We were sponsored by the World Council of Churches. That was during the summer of 1950. Louie worked in Germany and I worked in France.

Although the war was over, the signs of it were everywhere . . . the whole earth seemed to be nothing but rubble from the continuous bombing that had gone on in the last days of the war. Our job was to rebuild the foundations of destroyed buildings, to give people the encouragement for a new start.

In most of the camps where we worked we met former German soldiers who made up part of the labor supply for the new buildings. They were quite astonished by our willingness to work. Again and again we were asked, "Why—why do you do this?" They didn't always understand our answer, which was hard to put into words. . . . But we wanted to show our love for Christ *and* our enemies . . . because a young man who had reason to hate had been transformed by God's love . . . and because this love had touched us. The love of God in Ralph Hamburger would not allow him to gloat over the wickedness or the failures of others. . : . He had seen the Nazis' sins uncovered . . . he had *been* there . . . and in his own strength he could not forgive them. But his vision of Christian love wasn't his own—it was from God Himself—and it was God's *agape* love that enabled him to love instead of hate.

And Ralph himself? He worked in Germany and he was perhaps a greater enigma to the Germans than we were. To one nineteen-year-old young man, in particular, he just didn't make sense. The young man had been a member of the Hitler Youth, trained from an early age to hate the Jews and to consider himself a superior human being, godless and self-sufficient. In his heart he was still a confirmed Nazi . . . "Hitler was God to me," he said. He hated with a physical hatred which was expressed, in particular, toward Ralph, the former member of the Dutch underground.

"Why do you do this?" he kept needling Ralph every time he saw him working with his shovel to remove the rubble, piece by piece. "We were your enemies and you conquered us. . . . You should hate us!" His campaign of hatred was continuous and unremitting.

Ralph prayed for the gift of love . . . he wanted to love this young man as he knew Christ loved him. As the boy's words became more mocking, Ralph smiled and kept working. At every turn he met unremitting hate with unremitting love. And then one day the young man stopped to talk and Ralph told him why he was there. . . . He told him about Jesus and about the love that was greater than any of the horrors he had seen.

The young man listened quietly and went away. But the next day he came back, asking almost the same questions, as if he just couldn't believe . . . but really wanted to.

The day came when love triumphed over hate. . . . The young man broke . . . he threw his arms around Ralph and said, "You've got something! I want what you've got!" Touched and won by the same love that had overpowered Ralph, the young man became a Christian.

Today Ralph ministers in a church in California, and the young man—transformed by love—is a dedicated pastor in a West German church. Ralph Hamburger is the godfather of his two children.

Gossip, another form of gloating over the wickedness of others, can do untold harm. As James points out, "So also the tongue is a small thing, but what enormous damage it can do. A great forest can be set on fire by one tiny spark" (James 3:5 LB). Of course, sometimes the talk is true . . . and the truth must be known. *Not gloating over wickedness* is not a holy cover-up . . . but love doesn't rejoice when the truth indicts our brothers and sisters.

When I was a little girl I was taught to consider these three things whenever I was tempted to spread gossip: Is it true? Is it necessary? Is it kind? And the greatest tongue stopper of the three was the last: Is it kind? . . . because some things can be true and maybe even necessary, but very often it just isn't kind to pass them on. Gossip travels quickly . . . it enlarges upon the truth, in most cases . . . it manufactures evidence of wrong-doing where there is none. It is hard to resist, but it can be done if we allow God to deal with it. Gossip can stop with us . . . it can go no further if we absorb it rather than feed its insatiable appetite. . . . "Fire goes out for lack of fuel, and tensions disappear when gossip stops" (Proverbs 26:20 LB).

There are other things we can do with our time, with our tongues, with our hearts and minds. As Jesus advised, "Whatever things are good and lovely and pure; think on these things" (*see* Philippians 4:8 KJV).

One of my new friends in Washington is a great person—strong, honest and straightforward . . . yet gentle and very dear. We get together each week for sharing and prayer—something, happily, we both feel the need to do. Peggy (the name is not for real) is the wife of a congressman (for real) and this morning as we met, she shared an experience that gave me a little more insight into Paul's words.

One of the men who ran against Peggy's husband in a past election seemed particularly unscrupulous in his campaign methods. He spread malicious tales and even lied in an attempt to undermine the voters' faith in the honesty of Peggy's husband —which was ironic because honesty is a quality for which Peggy's husband is respected by supporters and opponents alike. That was hitting below the belt! The campaign was difficult and painful, and Peggy was hurting all through it. Even though her husband was reelected, she still felt the pain for a long time after the election. Then she began to find a kind of comfort in gloating over the former opponent's wickedness . . . it eased her pain and made her feel better to visualize him as the Bad Guy. (Strange, how much easier it is to feel we are *all* right when we see the one opposing us as *all* wrong!)

But life is rarely that tidy, and as time went on Peg began to hear some good things about the man who ran against her husband. . . . She could feel some good vibrations coming out of the causes he supported and some of the things he was doing.

In fact, he was involved in many of the issues that were near to her heart.

Because Peg is a fair-minded person, she had to open her mind to the possibility that perhaps this man was not *all* wrong as a human being. . . . As she found out more about him, her need to gloat over his wickedness began to disappear . . . and she discovered a man who stood for what he believed was right and what he thought was true (even if it wasn't always right and true). In short, he was a man who was able to be wrong—and able to be right—but always with conviction. "We need men of conviction," Peg said. . . .

As we reread Paul's description of the characteristics of love we came to: *Love does not keep account of evil, or gloat over the wickedness of others,* and Peg added, "And sometimes love means changing your mind about people."

Yes—oh, yes!

O God, if we are to love others as You love us, it will mean burning our stamp books and tearing up our ledgers of evils done against us. Help us to do it—now—so we can walk free in Your love. Amen.

9

*This love . . . is glad with all good men
when Truth prevails . . . .*

A Subtle Sin

A minister we know was preaching from Matthew 25 one Sunday morning and he made the point that Christians are to feed the poor, clothe the naked, and care for widows and sick. After the service one of the congregation came up to him angrily and said, "You stop preaching socialism from this pulpit!"

"Socialism?" said the minister. "That's not socialism—that's the Bible!"

"Then I don't like it!" said the man.

It's been said that politics and religion don't mix, but I don't agree. If the two are uncomfortable together, it may be that our political views are at odds with our faith. It should be the other way around . . . our faith should influence our political stands. It should give us the guidelines for determining whether we are being opinionated or open to the truth.

During the 1960s, when our country was going through a painful exposure to the truth about oppressed minorities, I'm sure there were many communities which felt they simply didn't have that kind of problem. In one of those communities, the black residents, according to many of the white residents, were perfectly comfortable and accepted . . . nobody discriminated against them . . . no opportunities were withheld from them.

103

And then, one day at a community gathering when many of the townspeople got together, a black minister stood up and told everybody just how angry his black brothers and sisters were—because they were held down by polite agreements among the whites. While there were no written prohibitions, there were unwritten understandings that kept them out of good neighborhoods, self-fulfilling jobs, and decent housing. No, they were not happy, comfortable, or accepted—and they had had enough!

Many of the white townspeople were indignant over this sudden exposure to the truth and they resisted it . . . but they could no longer deny that they had a problem. Meanwhile the anger and the bitterness grew, making it difficult to reconcile the two sides. Many relationships were strained, even shattered, during the struggle to acknowledge the truth and do something about it. It took patience on both sides . . . and a tremendous amount of God's love at work in all the human beings involved. But finally, when the problem was out in the open, steps were taken to open up the community—to provide housing and equal employment opportunities. It was a beginning! Only after human nature had been transformed by God's nature could love be glad that truth *had* prevailed.

In this day of constant exposure to current events, some of the news—much of it, in fact—is hard to take. Some of the men and women in whom we put our trust turn out to be less than honest . . . many of the resources we took for granted appear to be dwindling . . . threats of armed conflict are on the horizon . . . our way of life is undergoing rapid change . . . and the problems of today are dwarfed by those looming up for tomorrow. It's enough to make us want to tune out—and yet we can't . . . not if we are loving. For love is strong enough to look at the truth realistically and be glad that it is visible. Because it is not afraid to face problems, it can be objective.

In a large, delightful family we knew, the youngest child—a boy named Ronnie—seemed to be headed for trouble. He was withdrawn and paid little attention to his parents. He was always into mischief and past the point where it was cute. Loving him as much as they did, his parents were reluctant to consider the possibility that he had a behavior problem . . . he would grow out of it, they thought. But increasingly they lost patience with him and found themselves shouting at him frequently . . . and the little boy responded with great hostility.

In the summertime it was the family's custom to invite a foreign student to live with them, and when Ronnie was three years old a young English girl came to stay with them. She had a way with children and the whole family just loved her. One day when Ronnie's mother was scolding him for something he had done, the girl watched them intently . . . and then she said, "Are you sure he can hear you?" No one had ever considered the possibility that Ronnie might not have heard many of the words spoken to him.

Ronnie was examined by an ear specialist and found to have an obstruction in his Eustachian tubes that interfered with his hearing. Simple surgery removed it and Ronnie was sent home within a few days. He was a different little boy . . . he became cooperative, affectionate . . . because love had looked at him objectively, willing to see the problem and face the truth. That's when something could be done about it.

Human love is nearsighted, and when it must face a problem it often cannot see beyond it. With God's love in us, how different our vision becomes! . . . We gain some perspective. We see the problem—yes, most clearly—but we also see over it, around, under, and through it.

When Paul says, "Love is glad," he isn't referring to a *ha-ha* fun kind of feeling. . . . No, this love is not giddy. It's down to earth, practical, and it knows that once a situation is uncovered it can be corrected, improved. When love is glad, it rejoices . . . it tunes in to the potential for goodness. It doesn't say, "I'm sick of hearing about corruption in government . . . I've had enough about the misuse of power. . . . Let's just forget about it!" Love says, "We've got to know the truth, no matter how long it takes or how much it hurts. Then we can see what has to be done to rebuild ourselves as a nation."

The Corinthian church was one of Paul's most troubled congregations . . . its members were constantly finding fault with each other, paying more attention to their flaws and shortcomings than to the expression of their faith. . . . We get the impression, from Paul's words, that he was advising them to retrain themselves . . . to build new habit patterns . . . to affirm rather than to deny each other. While he was not suggesting that they blind themselves to each other's faults, he was warning them not to dwell on them.

A few years ago when the encounter groups became popular, it was typical for people to look for the weaknesses, the flaws in each other. While that method helped some people to become more objective about themselves and to be conscious of the effect of their behavior on others, just knowing that someone was angry with you didn't always lead to a better way of life. Some people became defensive under so much fire . . . they didn't like looking only at the things that were wrong with them . . . it was depressing, sometimes hopeless. Now many of these groups have changed their methods . . . they have learned that people find more stimulus to grow when honesty is based on affirmation and love.

For instance, when Jesus told Peter that He would build His church on people like him, He wasn't overlooking Peter's short-comings—and there were plenty! Jesus saw them all . . . but He looked beyond them, affirming an inner strength that Peter didn't know he had—until much later. That's what love does . . . it appraises the whole person, the whole situation . . . it sees beyond the obnoxious or the irritating . . . and then it works with whatever is good. For the truth is that there is a great potential for good in every one of us.

Frances Cooper was a high-school English teacher who seemed to see things in her students that weren't apparent to others. Over the years the principal of her school had discovered that she had a talent for bringing out the best in people, and so he always arranged for the so-called incorrigibles to be in her class. Somehow she was able to transform them into attentive, productive, confident students—how, the principal didn't know, because she was a gentle, soft-spoken, sensitive, almost delicate lady.

It seemed, however, that Frances Cooper was going to meet her match in rebellious, resentful, mocking Todd, a student on the verge of permanent expulsion for disrupting classes, smoking in the halls, absenteeism, fighting, defacing walls, and disrespectful remarks to his teachers. But off he went to Mrs. Cooper's class where he sat smirking, as if to say, "Let's see you take me on, Lady." Well, she did, and within a few months Todd's grades improved, his attendance record was perfect, and his conduct remarkable. Beneath the hurt, hostile exterior was a gentleman —and a bright, determined boy who was getting ready to take on a challenge.

When Todd graduated he couldn't afford to go to college and his grades weren't good enough to merit a scholarship. So he worked days and went to college at night—for seven long years. Halfway through school he married a lovely girl and has two young boys of his own . . . . and now he's a teacher. There seems to be no trace of the unhappy rebel.

The school principal never knew how Frances Cooper did it . . . whenever he visited her class, everything was in order and she was discussing literature with the group as if they were her close friends. She created such a confidential atmosphere that the principal felt he was intruding and never stayed long. But he wondered. . . .

Some of Mrs. Cooper's other students knew her secret. . . . My friend was one of them, and she told me that Frances Cooper had an amazing love that accepted each boy and girl wholly and unconditionally. When Todd glared at her, she looked him in the eye as if to say, "You can't fool me, young man . . . you've got a lot of good in you. . . . Now I'm just going to poke around and find it." And she did. . . . As she kept poking and loving, she began to build on the deeply buried strengths she found in the boy. Finding the gentle side of his nature, she built a sense of security into it so that he no longer felt he had to defend himself against his toughness. She built confidence into it so that he began to rechannel this strength into productive efforts . . . touching his vivid imagination, she encouraged him to dream about his future and what he might do with his abilities. . . . She stimulated his intelligence with interesting extra assignments that he could do in his spare time. Through her love she retrained his attitude toward himself until he began to see himself through her eyes. Out of her love came a new self-respect.

I have always been delighted by the story of Don Quixote, who saw beauty in certain people who, by the world's standards, had no beauty at all. . . . It's a charming outlook and I'm tempted to say that I wish we all could be that way. But Don

Quixote was not a realist—some think he was slightly mad, fantasizing and dreaming as he did. This is not what God's *agape* love does and it is not what we will do when we have His love in us. When we affirm something, when we build on the potential for goodness in a person or a situation, it will be because that goodness really does exist, however hidden it may be from human eyes. And we will find it because we are glad with truth and reality. (But I still love Don Quixote!)

I had a problem to discuss with a man who was working on a church project, and only when it was too late to do anything about it did I realize that I had approached him in the wrong way. I told him what I thought was wrong with the project . . . without first honestly mentioning how many things were right with it . . . and of course he became defensive. I apologized immediately, but the damage was done and I had the uncomfortable feeling inside me that I was doing things my way instead of God's way. And at that moment I realized that it is a sin to make someone unnecessarily defensive. . . . Yes, at least for me it is, because when I make someone defensive it means I am out of character with God's love—and that's what sin is all about.

We can't overlook some of the things people do . . . and on important issues we do have to point out the faults as we see them . . . but there are better ways to do it. I'm thinking of a wonderful man who helped my husband in a most loving way.

Bob was one of the elders of our church, and a *covenant* brother. One Sunday he had an announcement he wanted Louie to make during the service and he whispered it to Louie just as the processional began. Actually that isn't the best time to give a minister a reminder because he usually is concentrating on the service—and my husband is no exception. And beyond that, remembering details when he is suffering the labor pains of a sermon is not one of Louie's strong parts. So when it was time to make Bob's announcement . . . he forgot.

The service ended and as Louie walked up the aisle the first person he saw was our friend. Realizing that he had goofed, his first reaction was, "Oh, no! I've done it again! How could I forget when he just asked me to do it!" Emotionally, he was flogging himself, being harder on himself than he deserved, and needing affirmation badly. . . . Bob took one look at him and before Louie could say a word he threw his arms around him and gave him a huge bear hug. "It's okay, Louie," he said.

"I'm sorry I goofed," Louie apologized.

"It's okay," Bob said, "I love you *just* the way you are!"

It was a brief experience, but it meant so much to Louie. It meant that he didn't have to be perfect . . . that he didn't have to remember everything . . . he was loved for what he was, strengths *and* weaknesses. Now, that kind of affirmation is free-ing . . . that's love seeing the inner truth and acting on it. (It also took the pressure off—and without pressure Louie says re-membering comes more easily.)

Affirmation works wonders in families . . . . the best marriages I know are those in which the husband and wife build on the best in each other . . . the honest facing of weaknesses without the need to linger over them . . . no attempts to change each other . . . but rather a loving acceptance of each as a whole person . . . support for the direction each one's life is taking . . . an ability to share and take delight in the warm feeling that comes with the good things that happen to each. These couples are so filled with the love of God in their individual lives that they simply must give of that love to each other. . . . And while these things need not be spoken in so many words, the joy they bring each other is constantly communicated.

When one notices so many books on child care, it becomes obvious that parents need some affirmation, too. . . . As parents we all make mistakes (and what parents do *not* know that!). We aren't perfect . . . if we were, we wouldn't need God. But we do need God, and His *agape* love can cover a multitude of our errors. In spite of our human shortcomings, we can give our children a great security—and a blessing—if we let them know how great we think they are. It won't turn their heads—they'll thrive on it, and so will we. Just as we rejoice in the truth that God finds delight in us, our children will respond with gladness when we let them know that they bring us joy. . . . And if that is the way we feel about them, why shouldn't we tell them!

My neighbor's little boy was playing with a friend in his back-yard when his mother and I pulled into the driveway. He didn't know we could hear him as he tugged at his friend's sleeve. Pointing to his mother, who was getting out of the car, he said, "That's my mother . . . she's nice . . . she laughs when I do something funny."

Love . . . appreciates.

Dear God, may Your love at work in us cause us to see the truth in every person . . . and let our affirmation and love for the others in our lives help release that truth . . . bringing gladness to You . . . to the one released . . . and to the world. And about our world, Lord . . . may Your love at work in us make us strong enough to face the truth about it—and our nation— and sustain us as we throw our lives into the painful process of encouraging truth. Then grant us along with all good men the joy and gladness that comes when truth prevails. Amen.

10

*This love . . . knows no limit to its
endurance, no end to its trust, no fading of
its hope; it can outlast anything. It is, in fact,
the one thing that still stands when all else
has fallen . . . .*

Love for Today and Always

Several years ago I read a story by newspaper columnist and
author, Bob Considine, in *Guideposts* magazine which I found
hard to believe. Had it simply been the story of a woman's
love for her husband, I couldn't accept it . . . but it was an
example of God's love in action. . . .

The story begins early in 1950 in the Taylors' small
apartment in Waltham, Massachusetts. Edith Taylor was
sure that she was "the luckiest woman on the block." She
and Karl had been married 23 years, and her heart still
skipped a beat when he walked into the room.

As for Karl, he gave every appearance of a man in love
with his wife.

He was attentive, devoted, thoughtful . . . whenever he was
away on a business trip—which was the only time they were
apart—he sent cards, letters, even small gifts from every place
he visited.

In February 1950 Karl accepted a government assignment to

111

work in Okinawa for a few months. . . . It was a long time to be away, and this time no little gifts arrived. But Edith understood . . . Karl must have been very busy. As the months dragged on it seemed to Edith that the assignment was taking longer than expected.

Each time she expected him home he'd write that he must stay "another three weeks." "Another month." "Just two months longer" . . . Karl's letters were coming less and less often. No gifts she understood. But a few pennies for a postage stamp?

Then, after weeks of silence, came a letter: "Dear Edith, I wish there were a kinder way to tell you that we are no longer married. . . ."

Karl had obtained a Mexican divorce by mail. . . . There was another woman, a Japanese girl named Aiko, a maid assigned to Karl's quarters in Okinawa. She was nineteen . . . Edith was forty-eight. Considine continues:

Now, if I were making up this story . . . [Edith] would fight that quick paper-divorce, she would hate her husband and the woman. . . . But I am describing here simply what did happen. Edith Taylor did not hate Karl. Perhaps she had loved him so long she was unable to stop loving him.

. . . or perhaps the love of God was a part of that love. Edith could picture Karl's situation so clearly . . . a penniless girl . . . a lonely man who—Edith had to admit—sometimes drank too much. Yes, she understood how it happened.

The only thing Edith could not believe was that he had stopped loving her. That he loved Aiko, too, she made herself accept.

But the difference in their ages, in their backgrounds—this couldn't be the kind of love she and Karl had known! Someday they would both discover this—someday, somehow, Karl would come home.

Edith began to build her life around this expectation. She wrote to Karl, asking him to keep in touch about the little everyday things in his life. And so their unusual correspondence began.

[Karl] wrote one day that he and Aiko were expecting a baby. Marie was born in 1951, then in 1953, Helen. Edith sent gifts to the little girls. She still wrote to Karl and he wrote back, the comfortable detailed letters of two people who knew each other very well: Helen had a tooth, Aiko's English was improving. Karl had lost weight.

Edith's life was lived now on Okinawa. She merely went through the motions of existence in Waltham. . . . Her mind was always on Karl. Someday he'll come back. . . . And then the terrible letter: Karl was dying of lung cancer.

Karl's last letters were filled with fear. Not for himself, but for Aiko, and especially for his two little girls. He had been saving to send them to school in America, but his hospital bills were taking everything. What would become of them?

Then Edith knew that her last gift to Karl could be peace of mind for these final weeks. She wrote him that, if Aiko were willing, she would take Marie and Helen and bring them up in Waltham.

For many months after Karl's death, Aiko would not let the children go. They were all she had ever known. Yet what could she offer them except a life like hers had been? . . . In November, 1956, she sent them to her "Dear Aunt Edith."

Edith was fifty-four years old by then and it was hard being a mother to a three-year-old and a five-year-old. But she found it was worth the effort . . . fear left the little girls' eyes . . . their faces grew plump . . . and for the first time in six years Edith was hurrying home from work. Cooking was fun again!

Edith hired a woman to care for the girls while she worked. Being both mother and wage-earner left her thin and tired. In [a few months] she became ill. . . . She was in the hospital two weeks with pneumonia.

There in the hospital bed, she faced the fact that she would be old before the girls were grown. She thought she had done everything that love for Karl asked of her, but

now she knew there was one thing more. She must bring
the girls' real mother here too.

She had made the decision, but doing it was something
else. Aiko was still a Japanese citizen, and that immigration
quota had a waiting list many years long.

Edith Taylor wrote to Bob Considine who then described
her story in his newspaper column. Through Edith's love, letters,
prayers, and the petitions of others who were moved by her
story, Congress passed a special bill and Aiko Taylor came to
the United States in 1957. As Considine concludes the story:

> As the plane [arrived], Edith had a moment of fear. What
> if she should hate this woman who had taken Karl away
> from her?
>
> The last person off the plane was a girl so thin and small
> Edith thought at first it was a child. She did not come down
> the stairs, she only stood there, clutching the railing, and
> Edith knew that, if she had been afraid, Aiko was near panic.
>
> She called Aiko's name and the girl rushed down the steps
> and into Edith's arms. In that brief moment, as they held
> each other, Edith had an extraordinary thought. "Help me
> to love this girl, as if she were part of Karl, come home. I
> prayed for him to come back. Now he has—in his two little
> daughters and in this gentle girl that he loved. Help me,
> God, to know that."

Edith's prayer was answered. Several years after the story
appeared in *Guideposts,* Aiko, Helen, and Marie were making
a good life for themselves, living with Edith in Waltham. The
girls were leaders in their school and Edith wrote that though
"God has taken one life I loved dearly, He has given me three
others to love. I am so thankful."

As I said, I would find this story hard to believe if I looked
at it from the standpoint of human love . . . no woman could
possibly endure so much suffering and not be bitter. But Edith
Taylor was so filled with God's love that she was able to give
when she thought there was nothing left. . . . And by giving,
she received—not only a living memory of her husband, but the
children she had always wanted to have and couldn't.

There are those who think of love as a frilly, sentimental, delicate feeling that is easily crushed or destroyed. While this may be true of human love under certain conditions, it is not descriptive of God's *agape* love. His love is strong, tough—gutsy— and Paul tells us, it **knows no limit to its endurance.** God's love can take it! It isn't cloistered or passive in the face of pain . . . it gets out in the world . . . in the streets . . . and it does things for others.

George McLeod described this quality far better than I can:

> I simply argue that the cross be raised again, at the center of the marketplace as well as on the steeple of the church. I am rediscovering the claim that Jesus was not crucified in a cathedral between two candles, but on a cross between two thieves, on the town garbage heap, on a crossroad so cosmo- politan that they had to write His title in Hebrew, and in Latin, and in Greek—or shall we say, in English, in Bantu, and in Africaans—at the kind of place where cynics talk smut, the thieves curse and soldiers gamble, because that is where He died, and that is what He died about, and that is where Christians should be and what Christians should be about.

There is a cost to this kind of love. . . . In St. Augustine's *Confession* he speaks of the terrible pain he felt after the death of a friend. And then he says—in so many words—that this is what comes of allowing our heart to go to anyone but God. No one else, he says, is worthy of our love and devotion . . . only God will not disappoint us.

While this is true and logical in a sense, something inside me resists, in this one instance, these conclusions of Augustine. I cannot reconcile them with my Jesus who wept over the plight of a city . . . who suffered such grief over the death of a friend . . . and who said, with all of His life, "Risk all for love's sake."

Yes, love can be painful as well as joyous. Love—and you may be hurt. Love—and almost certainly your heart will be broken, not once but many times. But withhold your love . . . protect your feelings . . . and you will be saying *no* to life—and *no* to God.

The Penalty of Love

If love should count you worthy, and should deign
One day to seek your door and be your guest,
Pause! ere you draw the bolt and bid him rest,
If in your old content you would remain;
For not alone he enters; in his train
Are angels of the mist; the lonely quest;
Dreams of the unfulfilled and unpossessed;
And sorrow, and life's immemorial pain.
He wakes desires you never may forget,
He shows you stars you never saw before,
He makes you share with him forevermore
The burden of the world's divine regret.
How wise you were to open not! and yet
How poor if you should turn him from the door!

S. R. LYSAGHT

When love is deep—as God's love always is—it "bears our griefs—and carries our sorrows" (*see* Isaiah 53:4 KJV). We see this in Jesus on the cross, the highest example of enduring love. This is love taking it on the chin . . . for us! This is love . . . bearing all things . . . for us—voluntarily taking on Himself the sins of others. Only Jesus can do this for us . . . we cannot do it for ourselves or for each other. But we can open ourselves to Him so that He can live in us . . . work in us . . . reach out to others through us. With His help we can take whatever life brings our way . . . we can, in fact, look for the things that need doing without fear that we will be crushed by the opposing forces. Yes . . . love is tough! It doesn't feel sorry for itself. . . . It goes on loving even in the face of tragedy, overwhelming odds, defeat. . . .

Life in cosmopolitan Corinth was difficult . . . there were political and economic upheavals, personal tragedies, daily uncertainties, just as there are today. And Paul was pointing out to the Corinthians that there was a source of strength available to them . . . a power that could survive any crisis, heartbreak, disappointment, or defeat—not bitterly, but exultantly. It enables us to love when the loving is hard.

In Greek the word *hupomeinein,* which is used in this verse, means "to bear" or "to endure," but not in the sense of sitting back, stoically accepting whatever comes our way. No . . . *hupomeinein* describes the spirit more than the act of enduring . . . it means that we can go through the worst that happens and come out on the other side . . . with God's love in us, we can conquer and transform the most difficult situation. Yes . . . we sink down, very much like a cork on rough seas might sink under a big wave—but we pop up again with an on-top joy. We are revived, made stronger and more loving than ever. This is the kind of love Paul was describing.

I was visiting a friend in the hospital some time ago when I was sadly reminded of this ability to get on top of things—sadly, because my friend had not yet experienced it. She had known some bad times in her life and now—midway through a pregnancy—she was seriously ill . . . the pain of past events had left her distrustful of many people, and while she suffered from her aloneness she simply couldn't allow herself to be hurt again. . . . She was saying an emphatic *no* to life—and to God.

For some reason she had been a little more open with my husband and me . . . she trusted us to come at least within a certain distance of her heart, but that was all. The sixties were difficult years in many ways—for the church, for ministers, and their wives. We, along with many others, had gone through some rough water, which she knew about, but which I didn't want to mention there in her hospital room. And so we talked in the way a patient and visitor will do.

Suddenly she took my hand with both of hers and held on tightly. "How can you be so trusting?" she demanded almost angrily, like a mother scolding a child who had run across a busy street. "You've been hurt, too—many times—and you still trust people! How?"

It was true . . . I had been hurt . . . but I had also been healed, and this was what I tried to tell her. I had been wounded, but God's amazing love had replenished the damaged cells in my spiritual structure. There was no way I could have done that on my own.

Senator Mark Hatfield knows what it means to let God love through you. . . . Several years ago he took a political stand that was considered by some ahead of its time, and by others outright treason. . . . He was one of the first of our leaders to speak out against the war in Vietnam, and he did it in a time when the war was considered justifiable by many people. Naturally he received a lot of mail, much of it opposing him, and this he was able to take . . . but the most hostile letters—many of them beginning with "Dear Ex-brother in Christ" or "Dear Traitor"—were from fellow Christians who felt that his political views were at odds with his faith.

Naturally, there were some rough days for Mark and his wife, Antoinette, as the hostility increased and became more vocal. It was a long time before public opinion about the war began to change and reflect many of the views Mark Hatfield had supported. One of the roughest experiences in life is to be misunderstood . . . to communicate and not be heard—or to be heard indistinctly. It's a time that we cannot get through graciously without God's help . . . and evidently Mark knew that because today he speaks of the incident objectively, without the slightest trace of bitterness—in fact, with a certain sweetness. . . . He and Antoinette came through it, their spirits unbroken, their joy in life and in their fellowman intact—even deepened. Pop! *Hupomeinein!* This, to me, is a sign of God's *agape* love at work in a human being.

It's rather amazing, when you think about it, that Jesus left the keys of the Kingdom in the hands of a scruffy group of men who hadn't distinguished themselves in any notable ways. Though He had reason to distrust Peter, who denied Him, and others who behaved less than bravely, He continued to trust them. He went to the cross believing in them. Actually we couldn't have blamed Him if He had just given up on them. . . . But He didn't—and He never gives up on us . . . and we are just like those well-intentioned but often disappointing disciples.

Love never does give up . . . it's always on the positive side, prone to believe the best of everyone. . . . It looks for the good motive even when the action is hard to understand. Now, don't get love wrong . . . . it isn't credulous, or naive . . . it's no Pollyanna . . . and it sees all. But that's just it . . . it sees far more than you or I can see because it looks beneath the surface of a person. It's . . . insightful. Its vision is in tune with God . . . and it trusts what it sees. Yes . . . love believes all things.

A friend of mine had a dream I truly wish I had had . . . and I'm grateful that she shared it with me. In her dream she found herself in a large room to which there was only one door. As she looked around she saw other people waiting, all of them terribly distraught. Some were weeping, some were moaning, and their sense of agony filled the room.

Then the door opened and Jesus entered the room. Quietly, gently, He went to each person. To the man nearest Him, He said, "Why are you crying, My child?"

"Oh, Lord" the man said, "I'm crying because when I was on earth, I didn't live the way I really wanted to. . . . But I *couldn't!*"

And Jesus asked, "Why couldn't you, My child?"

"I was too busy trying to make a living, Lord. . . . I was so poor, I had to spend all my time overcoming it. I just didn't have time for You!"

Jesus smiled and said, "But didn't you get My letter?"

"What? Lord, You wrote me a letter?"

"Oh, yes . . . I wrote you a letter and I said, 'Consider the lilies of the field . . . how they grow. They toil not, neither do they spin. . . . Seek you first My Kingdom . . . and all the things that you need I will give to you.' " (*See* Matthew 6:28, 33 KJV.)

"Oh, Lord!" the man cried. "I heard that in church one day, but I didn't know it was for me."

"But it was . . . it was," He said, and moved on to the next person.

"Why are you crying, My child?" He asked.

And the woman said, "I've been so worried all these years. You know, my husband died a long time ago, and I've been all alone since then. It was very hard, not knowing what each day would bring."

Once again He said, "But didn't *you* get My letter?"

"No, Lord, I didn't know You wrote me a letter! For me?"

"Yes, My child . . . and in My letter I wrote, 'Happy are those who mourn, for they shall be comforted. . . . Do not be anxious for tomorrow . . . I will give you whatever you need.' " (*See* Matthew 5:4; 6:34 RSV.)

"I remember . . . the minister read those words at my husband's funeral . . . but I didn't know they were for *me!*"

"Oh, yes," He said, "I wrote that for you."

And as He went around the room, speaking to everyone there,

each person seemed to represent the things that hold us back from God—overambition, greed, sorrow, lack of physical things, pride, fear, anxiety, plus all the little things that blur our spiritual awareness of the nearness of Jesus. And in each case He had written the person a letter assuring him of the things he needed to attain a full life. . . . And no one realized that the letter was meant for him!

"Coke! Did you know that God has written *you* a letter?" my friend asked after she told me about her dream. And, really, as this friend always does—she made me think! The Scriptures *are* letters—personal letters from God to each one of us. If you want to open your mail, just read through any of the passages that begin with the word *whosoever*—and substitute the words "that means me" for *whosoever*. These are the promises God has made to each one of us. . . . These are His assurances that He will never let us down . . . that He believes in us . . . that He sees into our hearts and minds and knows that we are frightened, lonely, hungry . . . that He has courage, companionship, and nourishment for us. And we can take God at His Word!

A very dear woman who was a great inspiration to me during my early days as a Christian, and who trusted God—it seemed to me—with every fibre of her being, was asked, shortly before her death, "If you had your whole life to live over, what would you do differently?"

Without reflecting for even a few seconds she answered, "I would believe God *more*."

Love believes *whosoever* means "me."

Perhaps it is because love trusts that there is **no fading of its hope** . . . for hope is the mark of the Christian spirit . . . the mark of Jesus. Even when we fail Him, even when we offer Him no apparent reason to hope for us, He hopes on . . . and on. And so will we when His love is ours.

How very well Paul knew the power of this hope of Christ, for Jesus hoped for him, believed in him, when he was a bitter enemy of the faith and persecuted its followers. But Jesus saw something in Paul that was not visible to others, and He built on that strength—until Paul became the person Jesus hoped he would be.

And isn't it true that when we think certain things about

people they often live up to—or down to—our expectations? What we see in them is often what they become . . . and so it is important for us to look at our fellow men and women through the eyes of God's love . . . for love always believes the best about people.

A couple we know were unable to give a reason for their hope during a difficult time in their life . . . yet they hoped on. Their teen-age daughter was rebelling so strenuously that all communication had broken down between them. Their relationship became so frustrating, their disagreements so frequent, that for the good of the girl her parents arranged for her to live with various friends and relatives off and on during most of those troubled years. For some of the time she stayed with our family, and we could see how restless her spirit was . . . . but, oh, so full of potential! For years we all prayed for her, and then one summer she had a deep spiritual awakening. Jesus came into her life . . . and what a change He made!

We were having breakfast with her parents the day she came home and I remember so well the look on her father's and mother's faces when the girl described how she felt. She was part of the family again and there was peace in her heart. We were so happy and excited for her . . . yet there was no surprise on her parents' faces . . . . they simply nodded their heads matter-of-factly, as if to say, "Wonderful! We knew it would happen—we just didn't know when." You see, they had never lost hope.

It was the same with Cathy, a very gentle woman whose husband was an alcoholic for twenty years. How many times Cathy thought she could stand it no longer, but when she reached the end of her hope, she allowed God to replenish her. And the day came when her husband "got honest"—stopped drinking and began to rebuild their lives. . . . "She never lost hope in me," he says.

In every Christian community there are those who are hard to love, hard to hope for. They bring bitterness, unrest . . . they are the two or three who vote "No" when a wave of the Spirit causes everyone else to vote "Yes" . . . they undermine when they can . . . they rub . . . they clash . . . they hurt.

But they also are made in God's image . . . and they are brothers and sisters for whom Christ died. For them love knows no limit to its hope . . . it is prepared to deal with difficult people and difficult circumstances . . . being honest, yes—but always hoping that one day, somehow, somewhere, in ways beyond our "ken," love will crash through every obstacle and bring to the surface what is deep inside the person.

My special friend Pat lives with her family in a house on the beach at La Jolla . . . a perfectly beautiful setting except for those times when a group of young people camped down on the beach and kept the family awake all night with their noise. They were a group who partied rough, played loud music and laughed at anyone who threatened to call the police. I guess—without stretching the truth—they could have been called "rowdies." But Pat saw something beyond that. Of course there were frustrations, and times when she would have to ask them to turn their music down a little bit at night. But Pat really loved those kids . . . and her care for them as people was deeper than her frustration over their people-noise. She never lectured them or scolded . . . but she did pray for them and she let them know it. I can just picture her saying cheerily, "I'm praying for you guys!" And she *really* did! After a while the beach noises began to quiet down . . . and then the young man who seemed to be the leader of the group was beautifully, wonderfully converted. And he in turn began to work with other young people in the area, sharing his faith in Jesus, and loving them very much as Pat had loved him. . . . It was a spiritual chain of hope that was growing, link by link . . . because a woman looked at a group of "rowdy kids" through the eyes of God's love.

Every now and then I think, "What would I see in people if I had only one day to look?" I mean, if I had one final chance to size people up, what would catch my eye? . . . Would I see their little faults? Their flaws? Would their more obvious errors block my vision? Would I give up hope for some of them? Turn my back on them? I sincerely hope not . . . for when we withdraw our hope from a person, that's the worst thing we can possibly do to them. It means we're saying, "I give up," and when we do that we close ourselves off—not only to other people but to God.

If I had only one day to see people for what they really are, I would want to look beyond all the things that are so obvious to my eyes . . . all the imperfections and even the glaring mistakes in their lives. I would want to look at the inner person, not at the outer garments . . . I hope I would get down to basics and look for the good in each man and woman, because that's what really counts. I hope I would see each one as God sees him . . . for though we may say *no* to God—God never rejects anyone. I guess what I'm really saying is that I hope I would *hope*—because that's the best way I can say, "I love you."

Because love trusts . . . because its hope never fades . . . *love can outlast anything.* There is no trial, no calamity, no disaster that is beyond the power of God's healing love. Trust in this, Paul was telling the Corinthians . . . hold onto it when the going is rough. God's love is tempered steel . . . it does not give way, no matter how much pressure is brought to bear.

When a crisis comes into my life, that's when I realize how fragile is my humanity. I dig in my heels, I clench my fists, and hold my ground as best I can. . . . My family is there to support me . . . my friends warm me with their affection and help . . . yet I know that at a certain point of stress I will break. It's almost as though the harder I brace myself, the more surely I will be broken. Yet broken I must be, for that is not the end of the story . . . rather it is the beginning, the point at which I gain a strength greater than anything I have ever known. For "God's strength is made perfect in my weakness" (*see* 2 Corinthians 12:9 KJV). From the pieces of my being, put back together with a loving hand, comes the understanding that even calamity can become an instrument of God if I yield my brokenness to Him. And if I don't . . . I will remain a fragmented person, my strength permanently shattered, my spirit maimed . . . unable to be of any real help to myself or to others.

Some people have a lot of bad breaks in life. . . . It's true, some of us are broken many times over. Until we can yield these shattering experiences to God, there can be no blessing in the midst of our calamities. I don't mean that it's good to feel pain, because it isn't . . . nor do I mean that in being blessed we won't feel the blows . . . of course, we do—very deeply. But we are cushioned by God's unfailing love. . . . The hurt goes through us and the healing follows . . . we are mendable.

I've known few people who have been broken as many times— or as devastatingly—as our friend Karen . . . nor have I known anyone more beautifully mended by a loving God. Her life was like a fairy tale during the early years . . . the child of a happy, loving family who lived in a delightful small town where they knew everybody . . . and then Karen went to college where she survived very well the experiences that often shake up young people who have lived sheltered lives—she simply adored all the "different" people she met. Although their backgrounds were different, she got along with everybody. She also met Em, her husband-to-be, and they were married soon after graduation. Then came the house in the suburbs of a large city, a successful career for Em, and the birth of two daughters, Kristin and Michelle, two years apart. Karen liked being a commuter's wife . . . she enjoyed dropping her husband at the railroad station and rushing back to see the girls off to school . . . most of all she enjoyed picking Em up at the end of the day and being all together as a family in their comfortable house. Sometimes her husband had to work late . . . sometimes he had to travel and be away over weekends . . . but Karen didn't mind. As she put it, "Everything was going so well . . . everything was just fine."

And then came the blows, one after another . . . far more than any human being could take. Karen recognized vague signals in Em's behavior that bothered her. . . . He apparently carried inner pressures and burdens she didn't always understand.

Although Em made an adequate living, the financial strain of their debts seemed to get to him in a way that he was unable to cope with, and this worried Karen. So she went to work to help pay some bills. She liked her job and enjoyed the people she met. Then one day, after attending a luncheon with some friends, she arrived home to find that Em had shot himself. He died on the operating table as doctors tried to save him.

With two little girls to bring up, Karen tried to hold her grief inside her, and she did it very well. Em's insurance and a small outside income left to Karen made her financially secure, but she needed to become interested in something, so she went back to school and got a degree in education. As soon as she became eligible to teach, she went to work full-time, but eventually preferred to substitute so that she could spend more time with her girls. "They were such a help to me," she said. "Taking care of them was part of my healing."

One summer they came to California to visit Em's relatives,

and they fell in love with the sea and the sun and the warmth and the outrageous colors of the flowers. . . . There they stayed and made their home. The girls were growing up into lovely young women and Karen made many friends who filled her life with affection.

One weekend Karen went on a retreat with a group from our church—"just for something to do"—and was unprepared for the experience she was about to have . . . for quite unexpectedly she found Christ in a new and living way. Later, at a Faith at Work Conference at the church, she took another step . . . discussing a Bible verse with a small group, she suddenly burst into tears. "I felt something happen to me," she said later, "and all the bitterness I had been holding inside me began to tumble out. . . . Until that moment I never could admit that I was angry at Em. . . . Imagine that!—angry at him for taking his life and leaving me alone just when everything was going so well for us. But everyone helped me to understand that it was a perfectly normal way for a person to feel at a time like that. And it was good to get it all out of me and let the resentment go . . . then I could remember Em in a loving way. . . . I could actually feel the healing." Karen's brokenness began to mend the moment she let Jesus into her life and became honest about her inner feelings.

So often God prepares us for the blows in life ahead of time. He did that for Karen. All the friends she had made, her acceptance of Jesus and her dependence on Him . . . how helpful they were to become when she and her daughter Michelle were badly injured while driving their car across one of the western states. The car rolled over several times and Karen and Michelle were near death from their injuries. They were in the hospital—in a strange town, among unfamiliar faces—for three months. . . . But during that time they were held close to their friends by cards, letters, even visits from those back home. Karen says it was all the prayers for them that healed her and Michelle faster than the doctors believed possible.

So once again Karen was broken and mended, but in a very short time life aimed another blow at her. . . . Michelle, while driving the car, did not see an elderly woman step off the curb in front of her. The woman was seriously injured and later died. Michelle took it hard, feeling that she was responsible for a life that was ended, but in a remarkably short time she was able to forgive herself . . . she did it with the help of her friends who showed her that God Himself had forgiven her and could lift the burden of guilt from her shoulders. Again, Karen was healed as she saw her daughter move back into the happy, productive life she had put aside.

And then came the worst blow. . . . Karen's other daughter—understanding, gentle, fun-loving Kristin—was dead. It happened in another accident on her way home from a ski trip. It was sudden, unexplainable, final. We weren't with Karen at the time it happened, but our son Tim was. We had moved to Washington, and Tim was visiting Karen when she was notified that Kristin was dead. . . . He was amazed and deeply touched by the way she and Michelle accepted the tragic fact.

Now and then I have a chance to talk to Karen by phone . . . and we write to each other . . . and I have been humbled by the things she says. She told me recently:

> I used to think that life was a matter of fair exchange. You scratch my back and I'll scratch yours . . . you invite me to your house and I'll invite you to mine. But that isn't what it's all about. I'm just beginning to find that out. . . . Life is freely giving and freely taking, with no expectation at all. After Kristin's death, it was a new thing for me just to receive God's love through so many prayers from others . . . and in no way do I have to give this back . . . . and in the same way, when there is an opportunity for each of us to give to others—totally and with no expectation of return—we simply do it. This is the way it is with God's love for us . . . we just have to receive it . . . and give it to others. . . . There's something about receiving God's love through prayer that gives me terrific strength . . . and then, to be able to give it out to others is so wonderful!
>
> There are these three big things—life, death, and love . . . and maybe we have no control over life and death, but we do have control over love. I really believe that love is immortal . . . that the more we give, the more we receive. . . . I don't mean giving in a martyr sense or in an attempt to gain points. Love isn't something you can try to do—it just happens . . . I don't think most people are even con-

scious of it. It's just something that feels warm and good inside you because God loves you . . . and you can't help but give some of that love to others. It's His love that makes you do it.

People have said, "Oh, how wonderfully you're taking all this!" . . . but I can't feel that way. I don't feel I have any choice because God has given me so much. It just happened this way . . . and I thank God for His bountiful gift of love . . . . and belief in Jesus Christ.

I guess it comes down to this. . . . First we have to take love from God . . . and then we have to give it to others and receive it from others, but in a completely different way from anything I used to believe. It just happens without our even being aware of it.

A star is broken, and there are planets . . . a broken bud allows the flower to appear . . . a family circle is broken so that another family may come to be . . . and the body of Christ was broken for us so that we might live. All this brokenness is the work of love . . . and hope goes on because it knows this.

Love is, in fact, the one thing that still stands when all else has fallen. . . . Love has no equal as a spiritual gift. Tongues cease, knowledge becomes obsolete, wisdom passes away, as do all other gifts. Only love goes with us from this world into the next . . . because God is love. Love is stronger than death . . . it transcends death . . . yes, love is eternal!

Eternal . . . but not impossible . . . for this *agape* love is meant to be part of our lives now, here on earth, as well as hereafter. It is not beyond our mortal reach . . . it is the meaning and the mission of life itself . . . it makes possible our communication with each other . . . it enables us to understand what is going on in the heart of another person . . . it provides us with the spiritual energy to live our lives as He wants us to live—in spite of stress, without bitterness, seeking only to give more because we are receiving so much.

Recently I was deeply touched when I met and listened to Mother Theresa, founder of the Missionaries of Charity in Calcutta, India. In a way that is an inspiration to everyone who is reached by her—and honoring Jesus—she has merged herself with human suffering and privation. Her words "On Love of God" (from *Something Beautiful for God* by Malcolm Muggeridge) speak to me in a special way . . . perhaps because her life has spoken to me. There is something here for all of us seeking "a more excellent way."

> "Thou shalt love the Lord thy God with thy whole heart, with thy whole soul, and with thy whole mind." This is the commandment of the great God, and he cannot command the impossible. Love is a fruit in season at all times, and within reach of every hand. Anyone may gather it and no limit is set. Everyone can reach this love through meditation, spirit of prayer and sacrifice, by an intense inner life.

Isn't it wonderful that God has not commanded us to do the impossible! This love *is* meant for us . . . and for every day.

Start Loving

THE MIRACLE OF FORGIVING

by Colleen Townsend Evans

Biblical quotations in this book are from
the J. B. Phillips version of the Bible
except on pages 51, 60, 117 from the Living
Bible and on page 119 from the Revised
Standard Version.

ISBN: 0-385-03955-7
Library of Congress Catalog Card Number 74-18883
Copyright © 1976 by Colleen Townsend Evans and Laura Hobe
All Rights Reserved
Printed in the United States of America
First Edition

Guideposts Edition Published by Arrangement
with Doubleday & Company, Inc.

IN APPRECIATION

With grateful appreciation
to Laura Hobe,
whose editorial assistance
has proved invaluable
to the writer.

GRATEFULLY . . .

Ah, but where and how to begin? So many have helped, and so generously.

First, my thanks to my husband, Louis H. Evans, Jr., and to my father-in-law, Louis H. Evans, Sr., for their helpful ideas, especially in the theology of forgiveness . . . to our friend, the Reverend Herb Meza, the Church of the Pilgrims, Washington, D.C., for his willingness to share his collected illustrations and quotations on the subject of forgiveness . . . to our dear friends Helen and George Johns, La Jolla, California, who snip and clip for me . . . and to all the friends who have shared their stories and their lives with me.

Colleen Townsend Evans
Washington, D.C.
March 1976

CONTENTS

Dear Father,

May those who do not yet know the miracle of your forgiveness find it—perhaps through these pages—and let it work in their lives. . . .

May those who have already known the lifting of the burden pass on that gift to others. Amen.

I

EVERYONE NEEDS

FORGIVING

℃℅ There he was at my front door, the man I had been watching on television a few weeks before. Young, handsome, intelligent . . . a beautiful human being . . . and in so much trouble. He had admitted, before a Senate Investigating Committee and under the glare of television lights, that he had lied under oath during an earlier investigation. He had helped to cover up a crime. His name was Jeb Stuart Magruder.

"Is your husband home?" he asked.

"No," I said. "He'll be here in about an hour."

"Okay," he said. "Would you ask him to give me a call? I'd like to talk to him when he's got a moment." It was a familiar message for my minister-husband.

He smiled and started to leave. I couldn't help myself . . . feeling terribly foolish, I blurted out, "I know you! That is, I feel as if I do. . . . I saw you on TV!"

He stopped and looked back.

I had to tell him. "What you said was wonderful!" My eyes were filling with tears as I remembered the choked-up feeling I had had as I watched him. When one of the questioners asked him if he had lied out of misguided loyalty or ambition, he said, "No, what I did was wrong. Now I want to tell the truth." I could see him sit up straighter . . . and in his eyes there was an expression of peace.

"You know the old saying?" he said to me there at our door, " 'Confession is good for the soul'? Well, it is." Then he left.

During the next few months, as we came to know and love Jeb, his wife Gail, and their four wonderful children, we realized that Jeb had done much more than confess his sins. He had been forgiven—by God, by his family, and by himself . . . and this forgiveness eventually freed him to rebuild his life after he paid the debt society required of him.

"I almost envy him his freedom," someone said wistfully. "Maybe everyone could use a little forgiveness." A strange comment, considering that it was spoken while Jeb was in prison serving his sentence. Yet I knew what the speaker meant by it. She, too, had seen the expression in his eyes and wished it could be in hers . . . she was not free, although she didn't know why she felt bound. She was like so many of us who think we haven't done anything wrong, yet we just don't feel right. As the famous psychiatrist Karl Menninger puts it: "We are made vaguely uneasy by this consciousness, this persistent sense of guilt, and we try to relieve it in various ways." We suffer from a nameless ailment that keeps us from getting close to God and to each other—an ailment that keeps us from loving fully and freely.

Nameless? . . . Perhaps not . . .

" . . . everyone has sinned; everyone falls short of the

beauty of God's plan" (Romans 3:23, Phillips) comes to my mind. *Everyone?* Is that possible? If someone has sinned, wouldn't he or she be aware of it? *Painfully* aware?

"If we refuse to admit that we are sinners, then we live in a world of illusion and truth becomes a stranger to us" (I John 1:8, Phillips). Now that comes pretty close to where I live!

I remember how I felt when I first became a Christian. I was almost overcome with my awareness of God's love . . . it made me feel special, because, with all my human faults, I knew I was accepted, cherished. And faults I did have—I knew that. Still, they weren't the obvious variety. I didn't steal or hate or deliberately lie . . . and I had tried (in vain, of course) never to hurt anyone. So while there were imperfections in my life, I felt quite confident that I wasn't what most people would call "a sinner."

When I asked Jesus Christ to come into my life, I wanted him to change me . . . I wanted to become the kind of a person he could use to reach other people, because, as far as I could understand, that is why we are here on this earth. I wanted—more than anything else—to help in the building of Christ's kingdom. But first I had to be made over—just a little bit, I thought.

"Lord, search me, and let me know if there is any sin in me," I prayed, not really expecting to receive a bad report. Then, to my dismay, I found myself becoming conscious of things I would have preferred to forget. . . . Perhaps I had not exactly *done* something wrong, but neither had I always done what was right. Even when my actions appeared to be blameless . . . not so my motivations. At least, not always. I had been proud of being a "good" person. . . . I had been silent in the presence of injustice. . . . I had worked out my differences with someone who had hurt me, yet I wouldn't let her get close enough to hurt me again. . . . Sometimes, when I had been thoughtful and kind, it was not always out of love for a person but because I wanted that person to love me. I had forced myself to be patient with an opposite point of view, when deep down inside I was furious.

Even more disturbing was my awareness of my uneven relationship with God. Somewhere I had read that sin, in the biblical sense, has three characteristics: We rebel against God and refuse to accept his love, we turn our back on God and live in isolation, and we don't live up to the potential God has created in each of us. I had been guilty of all three.

Yes, as much as I found myself warmed by the new love I felt coming into my life, there had been times when I refused to acknowledge it. I still had moments of self-doubt. I still thought there were things about me that no one—not even God—could possibly love . . . and in that sense I was rebelling against God. At that moment I was telling him, "No, you may *not* love me, at least not right now." And when we do not love ourselves we are, in a sense, telling God that he is wrong to love us. How rebellious can we be!

Even though I prayed for God's guidance in my life, I still thought there were a few things I could handle by myself. So, every now and then, I went my own way . . . a very lonely road indeed.

As far as my potential was concerned, I was far from letting God work freely in my life. . . . I was not allowing him to stretch me and shape me. I just didn't realize that I—

along with all God's children—had a potential waiting to be reached.

Yes, I had sinned, and the knowledge of it made me uncomfortable. Because of something I had done—or not done —I had become separated, cut off, from God and from other men and women . . . and that is what sin is all about. I had asked Christ into my life, but I was not letting him express himself through me. I was still trying to live up to *my* standards of behavior, not his, and there is a vast difference between the two.

Once I began to think about the word *sin*, I realized that it is not restricted to crimes of murder or thievery or treachery, such as we might find in Shakespeare's tragedies. It is far more common. It is, in fact, a universal human condition.

Everyone, at times, has refused to be loved, accepted, and enjoyed by God. Everyone has insisted on doing things his way instead of God's way . . . and who has not fallen short of the mark God sets for each of us? Everyone has moments when he or she has been selfish, apathetic, cynical, greedy, dishonest, defensive, ambitious, joyless. We say we have our reasons, that it's an unpleasant world. Many of us are concerned with the wrongs we see in our lives, in our society, our government, our nation, and our world. Every day we seem to find more reasons to become angry, to hate and want to hit back at the hurt we feel has been done to us. And so we feel more alienated, more lonely than ever before. We know that God wants us to behave in other ways, yet we think he just doesn't understand how tough life is for us, and so we make up our own standards by which to live.

But now we are finding that we can't put things back together again with our hate. Only love can rebuild, and we don't know how to love any more. Something keeps getting in the way of it. . . . When someone hurts us, or when we hurt another person, we often say that "Something has come between us." This is where we are today—with so much between us and our fellow man and God. As I read somewhere —and cannot find the source again—"He that cannot forgive others breaks the bridge over which he himself must pass if he would ever reach heaven; for everyone has need to be forgiven."

A nameless ailment? No . . . it has a name and the word is *sin.* But fortunately, we have a Doctor and there is an antidote. If we will allow our Lord to teach us the meaning of forgiveness . . . and if we will make his forgiveness a part of our moment-to-moment existence . . . then we will be able to love again. The distance between ourselves and God and others will be closed, and we ourselves will be healed of the guilt, anxiety, and loneliness that plague us.

But first—we have to deal with that vague, uneasy sense of guilt . . . we have to be honest with the Doctor about the nature of our ailment. We have to examine the wrongs we have done, the right things we haven't done, and the unpleasant motivations that indicate we are not as OK as we think we are.

CHAPTER 1

"I Did Something Wrong!"

There are days when I don't like to open my newspaper. Everything I read is shocking, depressing, painful, or sad. . . . The world is *not* like that—at least, not all of it. Can it be that some newspaper editors believe they can sell more copies by emphasizing all the bad things that happen? Is this just a maneuver to get a reader's attention?

Deliberate sin is difficult for me to understand . . . it means that someone purposefully sets out to hurt someone else, and I don't want to accept that as fact. Deliberate sin is in the minority, I tell myself. . . . Of course there is pain in this world—and I don't want to hide from it—I need to be aware. But there is another side. . . .

And then I open my front door to get my newspaper and see the headlines lying there at my feet—someone has left a bomb in a locker in a busy airline terminal . . . it's the holiday season and so many people are traveling to be with friends and relatives . . . and the bomb goes off and kills and maims. Why? . . . Would it make any difference if we knew why? The fact is, someone intended to hurt and destroy other persons. Someone knew that what he was doing was wrong, yet he went ahead and did it. The enormity of the crime offsets the fact that it isn't the kind of thing that happens every day.

But am I right in making that assumption? We don't read about bombs going off every day, yet there are many other ways in which lives are destroyed—deliberately. When a person does something wrong—and knows it—he is putting his own law before the law of God and the law of other human beings. His needs come first—never mind anyone else's—and that can be very destructive.

Adam and Eve were like that. They were aware of what they were doing when they sinned, but in their minds their need for power was more important to them than the need to be obedient to God.

Well, now . . . that brings deliberate sin down to a level I can understand. I always think of Adam and Eve as ordinary human beings—not monsters of depravity, not terrorists. People like them are hardly in the minority, are they?

The realization makes me uneasy. If Adam and Eve were ordinary human beings—like me and like just about every other person I have ever known—then that must mean everyone is capable of deliberate sin. And conversely, it must mean that people who leave bombs in airport lockers are capable of behaving decently in some other areas of their lives. The acts of deliberate sin may be in the minority, but the sinners definitely are not! We are everywhere.

Some years ago, in a church we were serving, a very sad-eyed beautiful young woman began coming to service every Sunday. Because she was obviously lonely, many people stopped to say a few words to her as she made her way out of the sanctuary each week. She was grateful for their friendliness, almost hungry for their acquaintance. When a young couple invited her to stay for coffee one Sunday, she accepted shyly, and then eagerly. She lived alone, she told them, and hadn't made any friends since coming to the city. It didn't take her long to make friends at the church. She was a delightful girl—thoughtful, warm, loving, and generous. But still there was that sadness about her . . . it kept others from getting close to her.

One lovely fall evening a group from the church were going for an outing. The girl had been very excited about the event, so when she didn't show up by the time everyone was ready to leave, her friends were concerned. One young woman elected to stay at the church and wait for her while the others went ahead.

About a half hour after the others had left, the girl arrived, her face stained with tears. She was terribly upset. Her friend put her arms around her, trying to calm her, but the girl wanted to talk. "Please, let me tell you what I couldn't tell you before!" the girl pleaded.

And then it all came out. . . . The girl was in love with a married man who worked in her office. She had known he was married when she first was attracted to him but she didn't care. She was lonely and she had never known a close relationship. The man was kind, attentive, and appreciative, and for the first time in her life the girl felt important— loved. She began having dinner with the man, but in time they became lovers. In the very beginning he told her he would never leave his wife and son—but at the same time he wanted her. She accepted that arrangement. She would have agreed to anything in order to hold on to him, because she thought she couldn't go on living without him. She needed him—and that was more important to her than the realization that she was involved in an unhealthy relationship.

I don't know why she finally began to attend church. Perhaps she had an even greater need—for a greater love. But something began to happen to her as she sat in the pew Sunday after Sunday. "I didn't know what to say to God," she told her friend. "I hadn't faced him for a long, long time. So I waited for him to say something to me.

"I expected all kinds of accusations, but there was nothing like that. All I felt was love—a different kind of love than I already had. I felt lifted up instead of pulled down.

"That's when I knew I had to do something about my life."

The girl was uneasy. For the first time she could see past her own desperate loneliness to one of the persons she was hurting—the wife of the man she loved. She didn't even know the woman, and perhaps the woman didn't know about her, but she was hurting her just the same and she knew she had to stop. How? She didn't know. She loved the man as much as ever, and he wouldn't let her go without a struggle. She wasn't strong enough to break off the relationship.

The next Sunday was the day a couple invited her to have coffee after church . . . and there were laughter and conversation, genuine interest and warm handclasps. When she went home she knew that something had come into her life that day—and with it was a message from God: She didn't have to be strong—Christ had all the strength she needed—

she would survive the broken relationship because something would replace the emptiness in her life.

That night she ended it. She told the man how she felt and said she did not think she should see him again. She asked for his help and he agreed to stay away from her.

The agreement didn't last long. One night in the middle of the week the man came to her door, begging to talk to her. Overcome with pity and still very much in love with him, she let him in. He wanted her back, he told her. He still didn't want to leave his family but he wanted the girl as well.

The girl gave in and let him stay, but the next morning she knew she had to begin all over again. When the man returned a few nights later, she refused to open her door. That was why she was late arriving for the outing . . . she had waited until he went away.

"I can't go back there," she told her friend. "I don't want to see him yet . . . I need time to get over him."

"You can stay at our house," her friend said. "We have plenty of room, and you can stay for as long as you like."

The girl realized that God was already beginning to end her loneliness. She was about to become part of a wonderful, loving family who accepted her as if she were their own. Too grateful to speak, she threw her arms around her friend and held her tight.

Much time has passed. The girl, with God's support, is still rebuilding her life, and sometimes the process is painful. Her love for the man died a slow death—but she survived. She has changed her job, given up her apartment, and still lives with her friend's family. She is working at making friends and becoming involved in their lives. And, best of all, she has become involved in a whole new style of life with Christ. In accepting his forgiveness and strength, the "old things have passed away, and, behold, all things are becoming new!"

It is so important for us to be able to see beyond the person's wrongdoing to the person himself—which really is a God's-eye view of mankind. And since we are not religious do-it-yourselfers, we need God within us so that we can see others better.

For instance, Judas is a person I usually dismiss quickly from my mind because it is hard for me to come to terms with his betrayal of his friend. I would like to think of him as someone not really human—and yet he was. He was one of twelve men specially chosen by Jesus to share his life, to walk with him, to know his moments of joy and sadness, his delights and disappointments. So there must have been something about him that made Jesus seek him out in this special way. But it is hard for me to accept the possibility that someone so honored could betray such a confidence . . . although probably, if I had known him, I would have liked him, too. . . . And that bothers me, because if I can hate the sin, how can I like the sinner?

Perhaps that is the point Jesus was trying to make when, understanding the inevitable result of Judas' political activism, he forgave him for what he was going to do. . . . We can indeed despise the sin and still love the sinner—if we allow Christ to live in us and love through us.

When it comes to doing something wrong, how many of us can cast the first stone? We may not be terrorists or murderers . . . or adulterers . . . we may be the "little sinners" who justify our wrongdoing with the remark, "Everybody's doing it." "Everybody" is padding his expense account, taking home paper clips from the office, telling white lies, giving false information—just a little bit—on his income tax return. . . . "Everybody" is giving too much time to his career and neglecting his family. . . . "Everybody" wants to keep "those people" out of his neighborhood—and out of his schools. . . . "Everybody" cheats on his exams, exceeds the speed limits, and looks for ways to get around the law. "Everybody" eats too much, consumes too much energy, and pollutes this good earth. It's not our fault—it's "Everybody's."

I don't like to think of myself as someone who could deliberately do wrong . . . and yet I know there is that potential in me because I am human. Like the Quaker who saw a man going to the gallows and said, "There, but for the grace of God, go I," you and I cannot claim credit for the times we do not sin. The occasions are many and the temptations are powerful—much too powerful for us to resist. We need help. . . . As much as we tell ourselves that we could never do such things as we condemn in others, the truth is, we *can*. And we do. Whether our sins are large or small, monstrous or "human," seen or unseen, we commit them. It is our human condition—and on our own we aren't strong enough to do otherwise.

But Someone Else is . . . Someone Else can help us put another person's need before our own. . . . Someone Else can open our eyes to the fact that "everybody" may be wrong. Someone Else knows that, in spite of the headlines of our lives, we are not what we sometimes seem to be. Someone Else knows that there is a potential for goodness in each of us. He put it there—and with his help we can reach it.

CHAPTER 2

Who, Me? I Didn't Do Anything Wrong!

℮⁀ɔ I was meeting two good friends for lunch. Joan had already arrived at the restaurant and I met Mary Jane at the entrance.

Joan waved to us from the table where she was seated, and I could tell she was eager to talk. "Wait till you hear this," she said as we joined her. Her eyes were bright, indignant.

When she entered the restaurant she told the hostess she was meeting two friends. "Maybe they're already here," she said, looking around the room for Mary Jane and me.

"Oh no," the hostess snapped, "they aren't." She didn't even look around.

"How can you know?" Joan said. "You don't know whom I'm meeting."

"They're not here," the woman insisted.

"I think I'll look around anyway," Joan said firmly. When she saw that we were not there, she asked to be seated at a table for three.

"You see," she told us, "it's still happening."

"It" was something familiar to Joan because she is black
. . . and proud of it. The waitress, seeing no other black pa-
trons in the room, assumed that Joan's friends were not
there. It never occurred to her that Joan might have white
friends. There are laws against discrimination today, but
some of us still manage to put people down.

Mary Jane and I were shocked . . . but then "it" happened again, right in front of our noses. The waitress
handed us our menus and when she came back to take our
orders, she began with me. Then she skipped Joan, who was
sitting next to me, and asked Mary Jane what she would
like.

Mary Jane was quick to sense what was happening and
said, "I believe my friend will order next," and Joan took it
from there. She gave the waitress her order, and then Mary
Jane ordered.

The waitress didn't scowl, neither did she apologize. I
don't think she was even aware of what she had done . . .
and that was the worst part of it. As far as she was concerned she hadn't done anything wrong. She had simply
done her job.

Usually we think of sin as something we *do* . . . but perhaps we hurt people more often by the things we don't do.
It's easier for us to be careful about what we do . . . but, oh,
the things we leave undone!

I've heard—and I guess everyone else has—that when a
person is close to death, it is not unusual for his whole life to
flash before him. In an instant he becomes aware of things
he has done all through the years, many of which fill him
with remorse.

Now, I am sure that we all are close to death at different times in our lives, without even knowing it. . . . If we had taken that earlier train, the one that derailed . . . If we had been at the airport when that bomb went off . . . But for me, there was a time when I was near death—and I knew it. As I lay in the back seat of the car, speeding through Los Angeles traffic toward Hollywood Presbyterian Hospital, my life did parade through my mind, and in an incredibly short amount of time. But it was not so much the things I had *done* as the things I had *not* done that left their mark on my heart. People I loved, and had not told nearly often enough . . . people I wanted to be with and do special things for, but had been too busy to squeeze into my life . . . And my family—it would be impossible to describe the love and tenderness I felt toward them . . . and the intensity of my desire to be for them all God intended me to be.

I was one grateful woman when—some time later, after emergency surgery and after the miracle of new life and healing filled my body—I was returned to my family. From that moment on I became determined to put people before programs, to give those who are closest to me the priority they deserve. I found a new freedom—the strength to say No to all kinds of requests that were good in themselves but would ultimately keep me from being and doing God's best. It was a freedom I needed.

And so, when I came to this chapter—"Who, me? I didn't do anything wrong!"—a special chord in my heart responded. We hear much about the sins of commission—now, what about the sins of omission? Isn't it sometimes true that the greatest pain we can inflict is not by the things we do, but by the things we leave undone?

The playwright George Bernard Shaw, who seemed to have some knowledge of what sin was all about, wrote, "The worst sin toward our fellow creatures is not to hate them, but to be indifferent to them: That's the essence of inhumanity."

"The essence of inhumanity" . . . what a thought! Not many of us overtly hate our sisters and brothers—we're too nice, too civilized for that. We simply ignore them!

As I think about Jesus' story of the Good Samaritan, I realize that the really bad guys were not the robbers who left their victim wounded by the side of the road, but the admired and respected people who looked the other way as they passed by the wounded man. Their silence—the way they ignored the human need—cried out through the centuries, "I don't care!"

"Remember that if a man knows what is right and fails to do it, his failure is a real sin" (James 4:17, Phillips). Could it be that indifference is the true opposite of love?

Indifference turns people into things, into objects unworthy of response . . . and that can hurt. I know . . . it's happened to me. I remember a time when a woman and I had entirely different points of view on an important issue before a committee on which we both served. I tried to explain my feelings to her after the meeting, but before I could say more than a few words, the woman interrupted.

"Really," she said coolly, "it isn't that important. It doesn't matter to me." Then she walked away.

That hurt! I felt rejected . . . and yet, she didn't *do* anything. That's just the point—she didn't listen to me, she didn't acknowledge my desire to communicate with her, she didn't consider me worth her time. She ignored me.

We can ignore people in so many ways—we don't have to brush them off. We can even give someone plenty of attention—and still ignore their most important needs.

When I was a very young actress under contract to a motion picture studio I frequently used to see another young woman who was to become one of the great stars of all time. She was on her way to the top then and she certainly got a lot of attention from everyone. But what kind of attention? In an environment where beauty was almost commonplace, this girl's physical loveliness stood out . . . she radiated sexuality . . . in short, she was a knockout! So wherever she went there were whistles and remarks, some of them embarrassing—to me, even dehumanizing. One day at lunchtime she and I were walking into the studio commissary, and it was interesting for me to notice the different ways we were treated. For me it was "Hi, Coke, how are you?" and a few questions that indicated people were interested in who I was and what I was doing. I was a person. But for the beautiful girl standing in line behind me it was "Hey, gorgeous!" and the kind of comment that indicated interest in her appearance but not in the person herself. Years later, after several marriages and broken relationships, she took her own life. . . . Stardom had been an unhappy, frustrating experience for her because, for all the attention it brought her, she—or the person she really was—felt ignored. . . . Since then I've wondered—Can a person actually die of neglect?

Neutrality is a form of indifference. As someone has said, "All that is needed for evil to triumph is the silence of good people." We could translate that into "I don't want to get involved," a statement we hear often today.

When a young woman named Kitty Genovese was stabbed to death under the streetlight outside her apartment building in New York, thirty-eight people did not want to get involved. Instead they watched from their windows as the young woman screamed and the killer attacked again and again. Unusual? A rarity? People aren't like that? Well, more recently, a Philadelphia wife and mother was returning from the supermarket one summer evening around eight o'clock and she was attacked by a man in her driveway as she got out of her car. She screamed and struggled. Neighbors saw the man drag her for a full block before he pulled her behind a school building, knocked her to the ground, and raped her. Moments later the woman—her kneecap broken and her clothing torn—limped to the corner where there were several shops and lighted windows. She approached a group of teen-agers and begged them to call the police—and they ignored her! She went into one of the shops and told a salesclerk what had happened. Would someone please call the police? No one did. The woman's purse had been stolen by her attacker and she didn't even have a coin to make a telephone call. Bruised, in severe pain from her broken kneecap, she limped on until finally she saw a policeman and got help.

If a person is doing something wrong, we don't have to join him in order to help him in his wrongdoing. All we have to do is neglect to interfere. . . . After all, haven't we been taught to "mind our own business," "live and let live," "keep our noses clean"? Neutrality is considered a respectable—and respected—position, not only among nations, but among people.

Perhaps so . . . and yet I know that when Christ lives

within us we cannot remain neutral or indifferent because
he is not. If he were, he wouldn't have walked this earth in
the first place, because that required his complete involvement in our lives. But he could not close his eyes or his heart
to us . . . and if we are really his, we will express the same
kind of sensitivity. In the presence of wrongdoing we will
not be neutral. We will be objective, yes, because we have
to be able to survey a situation honestly if we are to be of
any real help. . . . And we will get very much involved . . .
because that is the nature of love.

"As for the well-to-do man who sees his brother in want
but shuts his eyes—and his heart—how could anyone believe
that the love of God lives in him? . . . Let us not love
merely in theory or in words—let us love in sincerity and
practice" (I John 3:17–18, Phillips).

Another form of indifference is neglect. We may love
someone but neglect to tell him, and that, to me, is a sin of
omission—a very common one. You can find it in the best—
and most loving—of families.

Most of us have been found wanting in this area. I remember one day several years ago when I attended a lecture by a speaker who asked an intriguing question: "Did
you ever tell someone you love that he or she gives you joy?"
I had to think about that. I wasn't sure I had—not in so
many words, and the words, in this case, were what mat-
tered. My husband and my children have always given me
great joy, but I couldn't be sure that they knew it—because I
hadn't told them. I told them I loved them—all the time—
but *joy* . . . I wasn't sure I had ever mentioned that.

When I went home late that afternoon, my husband was
in his study preparing his Sunday sermon. He was deep in

concentration, but I simply had to interrupt him, if only for a moment. "Louie," I said, and when I had his attention, I went on, "I just wanted you to know that you give me real joy!" Hearing myself, I thought he might think I was a little silly—but no, he didn't. His face lit up.

"Thank you, Coke," he said. "That's special—it's wonderful to know that."

When our children came home from school, I told each one the same thing, and the delighted expressions on their faces made me choke up a bit. My daughter Andie hugged me and said, "Hey, Mom, that's great—because you bring us joy, too!" And then I knew how it felt to be *told* that I was loved, even though I had hoped it was true all along.

You bring me joy—in so many words—is beautiful!

CHAPTER 3

"I Did the Right Thing!"

An elderly woman was causing quite a commotion on a busy city street. She was walking along with a sandwich board over her shoulders, on each side of which was this message: "Touch me—wrinkles are not contagious!" She didn't say a word, but as people passed her they turned their heads, struck by the words that so clearly described the isolation of the elderly today.

Until recently the elderly were a functioning part of our society. Usually they lived with or near the younger members of their families, helping to bring up children and doing many little thoughtful things no one else seemed to have the time to do. Sometimes they were ill, sometimes they stubbornly resisted new ways, and sometimes they seemed to live in the past, but these problems were considered part—not the whole—of being old.

Now that our society is more affluent, we are able to treat our senior citizens differently. We don't have to take them in when they become too old to maintain their own homes—we can put them in nursing homes. And we don't have to let them work as long as they once did—in fact, we insist on their early retirement. We build "leisure communities" where they can live together without the noise and intrusion of young people, children, dogs, or cats. Now, if this is their choice—well and good. But could it be, in some instances, that we are doing all the right things for the elderly—but with the wrong motivations? Secretly—so secretly that we dare not tell ourselves—we seem to be getting them out of our way. We are giving them our money, but not ourselves. That is what the old woman with the sandwich board was telling us.

Sometimes the nursing home is the only solution—but not always. Sometimes an elderly man or woman may not want to retire. And perhaps our older citizens may prefer the company of those who are younger.

Doing the right things for the wrong reasons is the most subtle of sins, and yet Jesus said that if we intend evil—and cover it up with acceptable behavior—it is nevertheless evil. The intention is what counts.

We have to be careful, especially within our own families, about our intentions. Are we sure they are what they seem to be? . . . We are quite capable of fooling ourselves, of thinking that our words of wisdom and advice mean only that we want to help someone we love. And yet, if we look a bit deeper, we find that sometimes we just want to help that person run his or her life.

We have four children—one son in high school and a daughter and two sons in college. Of course, we're partial, but we think they are great people . . . and because of their honesty with us, my husband and I feel that God has used them to help us see ourselves more objectively. More than any other people in our lives, our children stimulate us to grow and stretch. When we are together, there never seems to be enough time to talk about all the things we want to share with each other. We're amazed—pleased, too—that they genuinely want to know how we feel about the things that are important to them. *But*—there is a fine line between sharing how *we* feel and telling them how we think *they* ought to feel about their concerns, their interests, and their relationships. And whenever we cross that line, our children call us on it—rightly so! Sometimes I'm reminded of a prayer written by a good friend of mine whose little girls have grown into lovely young women by now—"Lord, help me to keep my hands off things that don't belong to me, such as other people's lives!"

I have to watch it with my husband, too. Being a natural-born fixer-upper, in times of crisis I am ready with all kinds of solutions to his problems—most of which he doesn't need. I tell myself I'm only trying to help—and in my way, I am—but the truth is, that kind of help isn't very helpful . . . and I dislike myself when I start giving it.

During the crisis years of the sixties, a reporter asked my husband for an interview, which in itself was no cause for alarm. But the newspaper for which the reporter worked was known for sensationalizing the facts, and in previous years had not been exactly friendly toward churches.

"Are you nervous?" I asked Louie the morning of the interview.

"No—should I be?" he said, smiling just a little.

"Well, what are you going to say?" I asked.

"I won't know that until the reporter asks me some questions."

I didn't want to put words in his mouth, but I "just happened" to have several things on my mind I thought he might like to mention. Before I could stop myself I was table-thumping about the progress the church was making.

Louie finished breakfast without a word.

"Well?" I said.

"Well—what?"

"Do you think you might want to mention some of these?"

"Oh, I think I'll play it by ear," he said, and kissed me good-by before he left for his office.

For the rest of the morning I fretted . . . telling myself it was concern for the way the interview was going. Then I began to realize that what really troubled me was not the outcome of the interview but the way I had treated Louie—and I fretted even more!

I had no peace until I stopped what I was doing and prayed . . . asking God to forgive me for slipping back into my old habit of being Little Mother Fixit. I knew that later I would have to ask the same forgiveness of Louie.

The interview went well. When Louie came home, he said, "What a neat guy! I think he can help me understand some things I need to know about our city. And, you know, he really *wanted* to know about the church and its mission in the city—about our people and their hopes and dreams for the future." Later in the week the article appeared in the newspaper and it was neither sensational nor derogatory. It was honest—even enthusiastic! And all without—or in spite of—my help!

It's hard, I know, for any of us to be objective about our intentions. So often we tell ourselves we mean one thing when really we mean something else. . . . The men and women involved in Watergate told themselves they wanted their man to win. . . . The person who doesn't want his neighborhood integrated tells himself he only wants the best for his children. . . . Those who oppose sending some of our food to hungry nations who are not our political allies tell themselves they are looking out for our national security. All of them feel they are doing the right thing, as they see it.

As they see it . . . perhaps that is where the difficulty lies. Each of us looks at the world in a different way . . . each of us has different needs, strengths, weaknesses, fears, and goals. It's almost impossible for us to agree on what is the right way for us to live. Each of us wants his or her own way, and all too often we are in conflict.

Motivations are tricky things—they don't like to come out into the open, probably because some of them aren't very nice. Let's face it—some of them are sinful! And for that reason we can't always trust them.

Getting to the truth may be uncomfortable. Jesus used to make some people uneasy because he was able to see through to the real reasons behind their behavior. . . . I can just imagine how Mary must have felt when she and Joseph, having lost track of Jesus in Jerusalem, finally found him in the Temple, talking with the teachers of law. I think I know what was going through Mary's mind. . . . She wanted her son to come home where she could take care of him . . . perhaps he hadn't been eating regularly and, like most mothers—I'm no exception—she was concerned about him.

Sometimes, when our children are old enough to go their own way in life, we mothers feel a bit helpless. We can no longer protect them from the hurts and disappointments in life, and so we put undue emphasis on the few simple things we can still do for them—we want them to come home and eat their dinner! Perhaps that's how Mary felt at that moment.

But she also was trying to keep her son too close to her, and Jesus saw that. "No!" he answered her firmly. "Why did you need to search? Didn't you realize I would be here at the Temple, in my Father's house?"

It was harsh, and I feel Mary might have been hurt by the remark, but I'm just as sure she also saw the truth her son had exposed. And for that she must have been grateful—most mothers *do* want their children to grow up and lead their own lives.

Perhaps, though, it's best if we aren't sure we are doing the right thing . . . perhaps we ought to let Jesus decide that for us. Could it be that it is better to make a mistake with a good motive—than to do the right thing for the wrong reason?

CHAPTER 4

When We Can't Forgive

℘ My friend . . . you turned away from me just now. . . . You don't want me to know there is alcohol on your breath . . . and at ten o'clock in the morning. Please don't try to hide. . . . Don't you know I love you—no matter how early you begin drinking? Whatever it is that drives you to drink before you can face the day—*that's* what concerns me, because it is destroying you. Why won't you let me touch you, reach you, love you?

And you, my other friend . . . why did you begin to weep when someone mentioned forgiveness? . . . . You still blame yourself, don't you? Your husband has been dead for six years and still you think you might have done something to save him. Why are you so hard on yourself? You did all you could. . . . You tried to persuade him to slow down after that heart attack, but he wasn't that kind of man. He had to move fast . . . get things done. You couldn't change that part of him. Friend, you didn't cause his death. You are not guilty . . . there is nothing to forgive.

Dear one, you have been hurt, and in the most painful way . . . by one close to you. . . . You loved her so and you thought she loved you . . . but that's all over now. She's gone. She loves someone else, or thinks she does—and you cannot forgive her. You do not even want to remember loving her because love seems so alien to you now . . . a distant memory, something for the very young to imagine. Dear friend, can't you see you are hurting yourself?

And you . . . will you never forgive them? Will you never put your trust in other leaders? You feel betrayed, I know . . . you had faith in their promises, you wanted to work with them toward a better world, and now you find that they didn't mean what they said. Behind their lofty vows they were petty, selfish, deceitful. . . . You resisted facing the truth for as long as you could, but now that you know, you refuse to accept the promises of other men. You cannot trust . . . don't you realize that cynicism is a sin—because it is the death of love?

There are so many others—troubled, guilt-ridden, unable to forgive themselves and others—carrying burdens beyond their ability to bear. When we can't get rid of our guilt or our resentment, we become separated, cut off—from ourselves, from others, and from God. We can't love any more . . . and we can't *feel* loved . . . so we take it out on ourselves. Friendships are strained, often broken, families are torn apart, some people turn to drinking or to drugs or to compulsive sex because they can't stand the loneliness that has come into their lives. Many of them are in hospitals or mental institutions because they—or someone in their lives—can't forgive and start loving again.

The apostles of humanism minimize sin—and leave us

frustrated because the pain is still there inside us and we don't know how to deal with it. As Vincent Taylor, the English Bible scholar, says, "The true friends of man are those who, while rejecting the doctrine of total depravity, see with clear eyes the sin in individuals and communities which is the cause of all our woe."

"This haunting sense of moral evil or sinfulness," Menninger says, ". . . usually has attached to it a need to be punished." Perhaps that is why a psychologist says that "Fear and resentment are at the basis of all neuroses," . . . and a woman who has been repeatedly hospitalized claims that "My body has been drained by inner conflicts of all power to resist disease." Our need for forgiveness leaves its mark on us.

When we can't forgive, strange things happen to us—in punishing ourselves we develop an appetite for failure . . . we become accident-prone . . . we lock ourselves into miserable human relationships. We punish ourselves in *some* way, for we are very resourceful. As a person sows, so shall he reap—but the crop is one of infinite variety. Guilt and feelings of hostility make it impossible for us to enjoy health —or impart it to others.

Some of us harbor a general sort of guilt. . . . Perhaps we didn't instigate the sin, but we helped to carry it out. Yes, of course, we were only following orders. . . . Sound familiar?

I know what many psychiatrists say about guilt—that it is undeserved, an illness of the mind, a figment of our imagination that can be reasoned out of existence. Yet I wonder about that. Some guilt *is* deserved. . . . If we do something wrong, shouldn't we feel convicted of a sin? If not, then we have lost touch with ourselves. No . . . some guilt is necessary, even useful. It can sound the alarm when we have done something wrong. It can lead us to repentance, to an honest facing of ourselves and our behavior.

Guilt is not meant to cripple us. Once we have experienced forgiveness, we are to carry the guilt no longer. Our minds and bodies should then have our permission to regain their health.

Why don't they?

How often we hear someone say, "Oh, I pray all the time —but my prayers just hit the ceiling. God doesn't seem to hear me." But he *does* hear. It is *we* who have broken the connection . . . because we can't forgive—and forgiveness is what keeps our line of holy communication open.

In Gabriel Marcel's play, *A Man of God,* a woman named Edmee is unfaithful to her husband. After months of inner struggle, her husband forgives her, but Edmee is unable to forgive herself. At one point in the play Edmee's brother-in-law describes her life-style, a life-style lived by many of us today—outwardly good, but inwardly burdened by guilt: "Edmee is so austere, so wrapped up in her duties, so absorbed in good work. It gives me the impression of a sleepwalker. I sometimes feel that your wife is going through life half conscious."

Half-conscious people—know anyone like that?

The poet e. e. cummings has another word for it . . . he calls it being "undead." And this is true of us when we allow guilt to rob us of life. We do not have the simplicity, the faith, and the courage to accept God's gift of forgiveness. We are afraid to take the risk of changing the way we live by yielding to his grace.

But why? Why do we not forgive others—and ourselves? Why do some of us hold our grievances so close to us? I think it was novelist John Steinbeck who wrote: "We gather our arms full of guilt as though it were precious stuff. It must be that we want it that way."

Self-destructive as that seems, I think it is true. Our lives can become like overloaded cabooses—too heavy for our motors to pull. And unresolved guilt is the heaviest burden in the world. It slows us down, exhausts us, decreases our abilities to perform our tasks . . . and on we go, dragging behind us our compromises, our wrongs, our neglect of those who need and love us—a lifetime of junk.

These are the things we can unburden—if we choose to be free, if we want to be healthy, if we want to love fully. Whatever keeps us from doing it?

I didn't really have an answer to that question when I came to this point in my thinking. And then I asked my daughter, "Andie, what do you suppose keeps us from forgiving?"

She thought for a moment and then she said one simple word: "Pride."

The more I thought about it, the more profound I discovered her answer to be. Our pride does get in the way of forgiving and being forgiven. It's an old enemy, but nevertheless a vigorous one, and we have done battle with it since Eden.

Of course—when we feel we are *so* right, and someone else is *so* wrong, we somehow feel justified in not forgiving—at least not right away! If someone hurts us, why not make him suffer a little, make him sweat? He deserves it! Yet all the time we are the ones who are suffering the most, because, in not forgiving, we are not able to love—*anyone*.

Anyone?

Even God . . .

Marilyn could not forgive God for the death of her husband. She and Paul had been married for thirty-eight happy years. They had been very close, and they had finally reached that point in their life together where they could begin to do the things they had always wanted to do. Paul was retired and they had more time for each other. And then, without warning, Paul suffered a severe heart attack and died.

To her friends Marilyn seemed very brave. They never saw her cry. But deep down inside she was in agony. When she was alone in the house she and Paul had loved—or when she walked in the garden he had planted with such enthusiasm—she wept bitterly. "Why did this happen to us?" she asked God. "What did we do to deserve this?"

Marilyn was uncomfortable in the company of other married couples. Their happiness was too painful to witness, but their discord was even worse. The slightest disagreement between a man and wife in her presence made her want to cry out, "Don't you know what you're doing! Don't you realize how much you have!"

One night, many months after Paul's death, Marilyn was awakened from a sound sleep. She heard someone calling her name. She sat up in bed and there was Paul, standing beside her. He looked exactly as she had remembered him.

"It was not a ghost or an apparition," Marilyn said, "because Paul took me in his arms, and for a while he just held me tight—in fact, so tight I could scarcely get my breath. Then, very gently, he said, 'Please don't cry any more. I'm very happy where I am, and I'll be waiting for you to join me.'

"It was so typical of him—hugging me so tight. I once told him he didn't know how strong he was and that he might accidentally break one of my ribs. He laughed and said, 'You just don't know how strong my love is for you.'"

Impossible? Marilyn doesn't think so—"Even though I do not understand how such a return is possible, Paul was recognizable in every way, even his voice. I am convinced that he came back to reassure and to comfort me.

"And since that night, instead of tears and regrets, or asking God why this had to happen to us, I now can thank God every day that Paul's passing from this life to a fuller one was not preceded by suffering, infirmity, and disability. I now wonder what I have ever done to deserve such a blessing."

We are just as hard on ourselves when *we* have sinned—or think we have—and there again the reason is pride. How can that be? Pride in hating oneself? Yes . . . there is a negative sort of ego satisfaction in punishing ourselves. . . . "See, I really *am* a bad guy!" Yet, when we say we can't forgive ourselves, we are telling God that our standards of forgiveness are higher than his—because he has already paid the price for our forgiveness, and it is ours for the asking.

I have seen pride destroy a family that once was warm and loving. There was laughter in their home, and such joy in the presence of children. But children grow up and make their own decisions, which can be a time of testing for any family. One child, a daughter, went away to school and, according to her parents, "That was the end of everything!" She had been a quiet, good-natured child, but now she enjoyed the company of boisterous friends who delighted in breaking rules. The girl was expelled from school, and instead of coming home she ran off with a young man her parents had never met. Her parents were hurt—so hurt that they made no effort to get in touch with their daughter. When she sent them letters, they tore them up without opening them. If she telephoned, they hung up the receiver as soon as they heard her voice. They refused to allow their other children to communicate with her.

A few years passed, and one day the parents received a telephone call from a doctor who told them that their daughter was in a hospital. She was dying and begged to see her parents for the last time. Trembling, the father said to the doctor, "You must be mistaken. . . . Our daughter is already dead. She died several years ago."

He hung up the phone. Tears stung his eyes as he told his wife about their daughter's request. His wife agreed that he had done the right thing. "I can't forgive her for what she's done!" she sobbed. "I'm glad it's over."

But it wasn't over . . . and it never will be as long as their pride stands in the way of their forgiveness. It is a sorrowful home they live in these days. No one laughs any more. The children are suspect—What are they doing? Where are they going? With whom? The parents can't enjoy a conversation with each other because they dare not let their eyes meet for fear they may read an accusation in them. And if they should, what then? Will they be able to bear the terrible guilt of what they have done—and cannot undo, because their daughter is dead?

No matter how misunderstood we are—or how mistreated we have been—we are never justified in withholding our forgiveness. Perhaps forgiveness is a road we are reluctant to travel, but we do not have to go alone. Wherever we walk in love, we go with God. All we have to do is take that first step, which begins with a prayer for the person who has wrongfully used us. And oh, what a weight will be lifted from our hearts.

Forgiveness is a gift, but it cannot be given until it is received . . . and we receive it only by faith. Simple? Yes! But hard!

Is there no other way? Let's take a look at the alternatives. . . .

We can repay in kind—the old "eye for an eye." No—revenge only assures the wrongdoer that he was right to hurt us and that maybe he should do a better job of it next time.

We can allow our resentment to build up . . . until it becomes so volatile that we explode—a slow form of suicide.

What about peaceful coexistence? Can't we just ignore the person? . . . have nothing more to do with him? But in order to do that we have to become insensitive to him . . . and that means we destroy part of ourselves.

Only if we have no need for forgiveness ourselves can we dare to withhold forgiveness from another. That's a risk too great to take.

"I never forgive," said General James Oglethorpe.

"Then, I hope, sir," replied John Wesley, "that you never sin."

Forgiveness and being forgiven—it's a two-way street down which we must walk. There is no other way to close the gap between ourselves and our fellow human beings. "If you forgive other people their failures, your Heavenly Father will also forgive you. But if you will not forgive. . . , neither will your Heavenly Father forgive you your failures" (Matthew 6:14–15, Phillips).

A family very different from the one I have just described chose to learn and live forgiveness during their time of testing. Theirs, too, was a happy home while the children were growing up . . . but then the difficulties began. There were arguments, disagreements about the way life should be lived. . . . Finally one son ran off to Mexico and a daughter went to live with a man by whom she became pregnant and had an abortion. Still the parents did not let go. There were letters from the boy in Mexico, and they were answered with warmth and tenderness. There were visits with the daughter, and sometimes she came home for a while.

"The most important thing to us was our feeling that no matter what our children did, we would always love them," the mother said. "And to us that meant hanging on in faith and hope and support—never letting go. To us, that is love."

When the daughter and her young man broke up their relationship, the parents helped the girl get a fresh start in her life. They arranged for her to spend a few months with a relative who lived in another part of the country, one who knew nothing about the girl's unhappy experiences. There she was able to get a job and adjust to a new environment— it gave her some confidence in her abilities. When she finally returned home, she was welcomed with perhaps some apprehension, but also with the willingness to understand. . . . Soon the son returned—still somewhat belligerent, but more aware now of the love that refused to turn its back on him.

This family has many problems to work out, but the parents have been sustained by Christ and the ability he gives them to forgive and keep on loving. As they saw it, they were passing on to their children the forgiveness and love God had given to them.

"The hurt, the distortions, the fear—all were there," said the mother. "I think I know too well what they look like. They nipped at me from all sides. But always there was Christ's promise: 'No matter what, I love you.' That became the banner we carried for our children. It reminded us that the *what* can never become more important than the *who*— and they are such beautiful *who's*."

It is not easy to be forgiven, or forgiving. Once we accept God's love for us we are challenged to let him reshape our lives. We have to face our sins and allow him to take them from us, and once that happens we can never be the same again—because as we discover our real selves beneath all those layers of guilt, we will begin to change and move out in new directions.

In a novel that was popular a few years ago, one of the characters made a statement that became quite famous: "Love means you never have to say you're sorry." Well, I'm afraid I have to disagree. For me, love means you *do* say you're sorry. . . . You don't hit the bottle, pull the trigger, become unbearable with those close to you, or bore people with your cynicism. You face what you have done and you repent . . . and then you allow God to love you back to health. You realize, as Sören Kierkegaard expressed it, that "I must repent myself back into the family, into the clan, into the race, back to God."

Love also means that when someone else is sorry, we accept his repentance and heal the breach with our continued love. "Let there be no more resentment, no more anger or temper. . . . Be kind to one another; be understanding. Be as ready to forgive others as God for Christ's sake has forgiven you" (Ephesians 4:31–32, Phillips).

A young woman—a friend of mine—who recently found a new relationship with Jesus Christ, shared with me her struggle to attain a forgiving love for those who had hurt her—and those close to her:

"Ruth Graham (Mrs. Billy) once told me that new Christians are like babies: Their new life in Christ is just beginning. Those words have great meaning to me, for, as one who has attempted to live the Christian life for just two years now, I have often felt vulnerable and discouraged in my faith and in need of an all-encompassing love, just as infants need care and love. What has sustained me in my faith is the overwhelming conviction I have whenever I read in the Bible that I am a "child of God"; and that God loves me unconditionally. I think often of the words in Colossians 3:13 (Living Bible):

"'Be gentle and ready to forgive; never hold grudges. Remember, the Lord forgave you, so you must forgive others.'

"Although only 26, two years ago I felt mentally middle-aged. I found that holding grudges and allowing bitterness to fester mutilated my spirit. With my new faith in Christ, however, I feel a sense of relief in shedding the attitude of criticism and constant judging of others.

"In John one reads 'God is love.' In my own life I have found these words to be true, and cherish the beautiful message, 'Most of all let love guide your life.'"

The young woman is Julie Nixon Eisenhower.

Make no mistake about it, forgiveness can be very

difficult. And yet we know that Christ wants us to forgive—so it must be for our own good. It must be that he loves us so much that he doesn't want us to be crippled by our harbored hurts—he wants to save us from the ills that plague us when we cannot love, from the guilt that entraps and entangles us when we will not admit we were wrong.

God wants us to walk free—liberated from our "guilted cage," as Lloyd Ogilvie calls it, no longer driven to please everybody—not even God—because we will know that we are already pleasing and do not have to earn our way to love, liberated from our hostilities and defensiveness, able to concentrate on loving and serving out of the joyous, healthy overflow of our fulfilled lives.

II

WHERE DOES GOD
COME IN?

A few minutes ago I hung up the phone after having a wonderful, warm visit with my friend Pat, three thousand miles away in California. She gave me a gift today—a bit of herself—her humor, her interest, her love. We shared a few laughs, a tear or two, our concerns . . . and then a prayer.

Now, as I sit here, nourished by our conversation, I realize "What a good friend Pat is! How I love talking to her!" We could have gone on for an hour—and I would have, except that it was her dime, and my conscience began pricking me. I feel so fortunate to have someone like Pat in my life, someone who loves me, someone who has said, with her life as well as her words, "Nothing you can do or say will ever come between us. I am committed to you—you are my friend."

This is the kind of relationship God wants to have with each one of us. He has told us in so many words: "I shall not call you servants any longer, for a servant does not share his master's confidence. No, I call you friends. . . ." (John 15:15, Phillips). He has said he will be nearer to us than our breathing, closer than our hands and feet. He wants us to share every level of our lives with him—our laughter and joys, our heartbreak and hardships. . . . And when we have sinned, he wants us to tell him what we have done. He wants to know all about it—*from us!* No matter what it is, he can take it. "There is only one God, and only one intermediary between God and men, the Man Jesus Christ. He gave himself as a ransom for us all—an act of redemption which happened once, but which stands for all time as a witness to what he is" (I Timothy 2:5–6, Phillips).

When it comes to forgiveness, we can go to the man at the top. . . . He is the One—the only One—who can deal with our sins . . . "For the son of Man has power on earth to forgive sins" (Matthew 9:6, Phillips). "If we confess our sins, he is faithful and just, and will forgive our sins and cleanse us from all unrighteousness" (I John 1:9, RSV). And he will forgive anyone—*anything.*

CHAPTER 5

Let's Get It Straight
What Is God Like?

℘ I was horrified. Lying there in pain in her hospital bed, she looked up at me and said, "I know why this has happened to me—God is punishing me for my sins."

"Oh no!" I said. "God isn't like that!"

Silently she shook her head—her mind was made up. Not that she protested—far from it. She thought she deserved to be punished. . . . This was the way she thought God dealt with sin.

How wrong she was. That was not God destroying her body, making her writhe in agony . . . that was not Christ telling her she was evil . . . that was the Accuser.

I have known him. We all have known him. He is always right there the moment we do something wrong, waiting to rub our noses in it, pointing his long, ugly finger at us, laughing as we squirm. "*You*," he tells us, "*you* did it! *You* committed this sin—and you shall suffer for it." If he has his way, we will suffer for the rest of our lives.

Let's come to an understanding right now—the Accuser is a clever impostor. The worst sin he commits is to insinuate that he speaks for God. He does not. He knows nothing of love. Forgiveness is his enemy, because once it is given and accepted, the Accuser is no more. Poof! He's gone!

The only time the Accuser has any power over us is when we do not—or feel we cannot—accept God's love and forgiveness in our lives. The moment we feel that we have done something so terrible that God will never forgive us, the Accuser makes his appearance. Oh, how he loves to take advantage of our self-doubts! Oh, how he tries to make us do unto others as he has done unto us. Feeling unloved and unforgiven, we become unloving—and unforgiving.

So, if you think you have asked for forgiveness and been denied, if your sins are dragged again and again into your consciousness, don't blame God. Your discomfort doesn't come from him, but from the Accuser.

How can we tell the difference? That's easy. God does not enjoy our discomfort—he does not want us to suffer. When we do—and when we go to him for forgiveness and healing—he soothes us and eases our pain. He knows that sin is excruciating, and that is why he offers us his immediate forgiveness. Not only that—he continues the relationship. He doesn't say, "I forgive you, but I want no more to do with you." He is always there, even when *we* turn away—and when we are reconciled to him, he receives us as a loving Father, not as an accusing judge.

While there is no sin God cannot forgive, his love is not a holy cover-up. Nor is he a pushover. When we feel God's forgiving mercy in our lives, we are not to withhold that same mercy from others. . . . But that doesn't mean we are to wink at evil. Forgiveness does not allow a fool to persist in folly . . . or lies to go unchallenged . . . or prejudice to flourish unopposed. Forgiveness is reality dealing sensibly with reality—love with a rugged face.

Forgiveness is free—to us—but it cost God dearly. So it is not free and easy!

Before Jesus paid the price of forgiveness on the cross, he told a very practical story about indebtedness. He wanted to be sure we understood what forgiveness is all about.

The setting for the story was the house of Simon the Pharisee, where Jesus had been invited for dinner. Simon was the kind of person my children might call "straight." He and his household were extremely proper and, I suspect, more than a little rigid.

While Simon and his guests were eating dinner, something unexpected happened, something that probably embarrassed Simon greatly. In from the streets stepped a prostitute—a woman to whom sin was not an occasional error, but a way of life. As Simon watched in shocked amazement at this intrusion into his orderly home, a remarkable event took place. As the woman stood before Christ—who was as relaxed as Simon was tense in her presence—she broke into tears. Apparently she saw something in Jesus that was so different from other men—a kindness, a love without lust— perhaps no one had ever looked at her as a person. And she was shaken. In a spontaneous gesture of holy affection and generosity, she washed his feet with tears and kisses, and dried them with her hair. Then she anointed them with a precious ointment which she had brought in an alabaster box.

Jesus accepted the act for what it was—a gift of love. But

Simon was incensed. Disgusted, he said to himself, "This proves that Jesus is no prophet, for if God had really sent him, he would know what kind of woman this one is!" (Luke 7:39 ff., Living Bible).

Jesus, knowing Simon's mind, decided to set him—and the record—straight. "Simon," he said, "I have something to say to you."

And then he told this story. . . .

"A man loaned money to two people—$5,000 to one and $500 to the other. But neither of them could pay him back, so he kindly forgave them both, letting them keep the money! Which do you suppose loved him most after that?"

Jesus did not answer his own question, as we so often do. He left it to Simon, who said, "I suppose the one who had owed him the most."

Jesus was not taking the woman's sin lightly. He was affirming her—not because she had sinned, but because she knew she had sinned and she came to the One who could do something about it. That was the kind of attitude to which he could respond.

The woman's sin had been born of a hunger for love—erroneous love, destructive love, to be sure—but when she saw the real thing in the eyes of Jesus, she recognized it . . . she wanted that kind of love in her life.

Her feelings for Jesus ran deep . . . and she did something about them. Simon was rigid . . . interested in Jesus, curious, perhaps, but holding him off at a skeptic's arm's length. So he did nothing.

Jesus went on with his story. "See this woman kneeling here! When I entered your home, you didn't bother to offer me water to wash the dust from my feet, but she has washed them with her tears and wiped them with her hair.

"You refused me the customary kiss of greeting, but she has kissed my feet again and again from the time I first came in.

"You neglected the usual courtesy of olive oil to anoint my head, but she has covered my feet with rare perfume. Therefore her sins—and they are many—are forgiven, for she loved me much; but one who is forgiven little, shows little love."

What kind of a God do we have? A loving God . . . one who is greater than all our sins . . . a truthful God who is patient with our weakness, generous with his strength . . . a God who wants to live in fellowship with us, his people . . . who wants to reconcile us to him no matter what we have done . . . and yet he respects our freedom and will.

This is the God to whom we can go at any time. No one stands in our way—except, perhaps, ourselves.

CHAPTER 6

God Has to Get into the Act

๛ Two middle-aged Dutch women . . . compassionate Christians caught up in a merciless war . . . arrested by the Nazis for hiding Jews in their home . . . sent to a concentration camp which only one of them survived. The story is familiar to many of us who have read *The Hiding Place* or known its author, Corrie Ten Boom. Her name is synonymous with forgiveness.

Humiliation, deprivation, hunger, brutality, nightmarish fear and shock, the slow, agonized death of a younger sister—not many of us are called upon to forgive such inhumanity. And yet Corrie Ten Boom's faith was so strengthened in the midst of suffering that she was able to return to Germany after World War II and tell the German people that God would forgive them their sins.

It was during one of her postwar lecture tours that Corrie Ten Boom was confronted by a man she recognized as one of the guards she had seen at Ravensbrück, the concentration camp where she and her sister were interned for several years. He came to speak to her after she had addressed a group in a church basement in Munich. He was now a Christian. He was thankful for her message to the German people, he said, but he had come to ask for Corrie's personal forgiveness. He offered her his hand.

". . . I stood there," she wrote, "I whose sins had every day to be forgiven—and could not."

During the next few seconds Corrie Ten Boom struggled with something more difficult than she had ever had to face. "For I had to do it—I knew that. The message that God forgives has a prior condition: that we forgive those who have injured us." In her home in Holland, where she had cared for many other victims of Nazi oppression, she saw that "Those who were able to forgive their former enemies were able also to return to the outside world and rebuild their lives, no matter what the physical scars. Those who nursed their bitterness remained invalids. It was as simple and as horrible as that."

And yet she could not give her hand to her former captor —until she asked Jesus for help. "'I can lift my hand. I can do that much,'" she prayed. "'You supply the feeling.'"

Awkwardly, feeling no love in her heart, she lifted her arm and held out her hand. "And as I did, an incredible thing took place. The current started in my shoulder, raced down my arm, sprang into our joined hands. And then this healing warmth seemed to flood my whole being, bringing tears to my eyes.

"'I forgive you, brother!' I cried. 'With all my heart!'"

I don't think I could have done what Corrie Ten Boom did . . . in fact, I *know* I couldn't! But then, neither could Corrie Ten Boom. She makes it quite clear that it was Christ himself who did the forgiving . . . it was his indestructible, unconditional love that vibrated through her, overcoming the very understandable human inability to deal with so much pain.

And the former guard—what about him? Imagine the guilt he carried with him as he walked to the front of the room to meet the woman he had abused so cruelly. How many deaths had he caused, how many lives had he crippled, how many minds had he driven to the point of madness! Would he ever be able to forget? Certainly, for-giveness—of himself or by others—must have seemed impos-sible.

But then, forgiveness is always impossible for us—for *all* of us, no matter whether the sin and guilt are great or small. We can't handle it ourselves, yet, oh, how we try!

A chaplain at a home for unwed mothers was counseling a young woman who kept saying over and over, "When I have my child, I hope my labor pains will be good and hard!" As if the rhythmic pains of birth could help her deal with her guilt.

Of course, they couldn't—but God can! God has to get into the act or there will be no forgiveness—only punish-ment.

I have known Mary Ann for a long time, but only recently did she really allow us to become friends. It seemed to me we had always wanted to be close, but around Mary Ann there was an invisible wall that kept people out. She had been married and divorced twice, and although I had never met either of her husbands, I sensed that they, too, had never been allowed to know who she was.

Mary Ann was a very helpful person and we had spent

many hours together working on a favorite community project. She had a delightful sense of humor, but sometimes right in the middle of her laughter, her eyes would suddenly look very sad—it was as if a cloud had passed in front of the sun and a shadow fell on the earth.

When we moved away from California I didn't see Mary Ann for several months. Then she came East for a visit . . . and the moment I met her at the airport I could see that she had changed. She came toward me with such eagerness. She took my hands in both of hers and held them tight. For a moment we both just grinned, and then we threw our arms around each other. Tears began to fill our eyes.

Now, I cry very easily, so there was nothing strange about that. . . . But I had never known Mary Ann to shed a tear—in sadness or in joy. Something had happened in her life!

My husband was away on a short speaking trip, so that evening Mary Ann and I sat up much too late, but for, oh, what a wonderful purpose! We shared, we laughed, we prayed. We thanked God for Mary Ann's discovery of herself. . . . It had happened a few weeks before she came to visit. . . .

Mary Ann had met a man named Hal, whom she admired very much. Hal also was attracted to her, so they began to see quite a lot of each other. He was a widower, with two grown children. She had had no children from either of her marriages. Sometimes, when they went out to dinner, they arranged to meet with the man's children, which was very pleasant for Mary Ann, who liked young people.

One night on their way home from the theater, Hal told Mary Ann that he would like to be married again. What did she think of the idea? Mary Ann felt herself grow cold, almost shivering. She tried to change the subject, but Hal finally came right out and asked her to marry him. Mary Ann said she would think about it.

She was awake all that night, trying to understand why she was so frightened. Hal had given her no reason to be afraid. He was a gentle, considerate, loving person. Mary Ann did not want to hurt him, yet she also did not want to see him again.

Puzzled, angry, not knowing where to turn, Mary Ann began to pray. She asked God to help her find the reason for her fear—not only of Hal, but of almost everyone she knew. "Why can't I get close to anyone?" she asked.

Toward morning, she was still praying. As she knelt, exhausted, by her bed, she saw the first streaks of light in the sky, and suddenly that same glow seemed to penetrate her whole being. The dark corners of her memory were gradually exposed and she began to recall something she had hidden from her consciousness many years ago.

When Mary Ann was fifteen years old—a slight, trusting, soft-spoken girl—a terrible thing had happened to her. As a joke—if anyone could call it that—a group of older boys tricked her into a storage room in the school basement, and there they raped her. Before they let her go they told her that if she ever told anyone about what happened, they would hurt her even more.

Mary Ann made her way home—stunned, sickened, and very ashamed. She could not tell her family—or anyone— about the attack. She was too embarrassed and frightened. She believed the boys would make good their threat. So, each day, for the rest of that year, she went to school where she saw the boys in the corridors and in some of her classes, and each day her fear and rage and shame deepened. Finally, to spare herself further agony, she "forgot" what happened—but only part of her mind wiped out the memory. The rest—the deep, inner reaches of her mind—remembered by sounding an alarm whenever anyone tried to get close to her. She was terrified of being hurt, of being truly known.

When Mary Ann was able to face what had happened to her, she was filled with hatred for the boys who had raped her. Forgive? No, she knew she could never forgive them! But how could she go on living with her rage? That, too, was a barrier to loving relationships.

"I had to ask God to do it for me," she told me. "And he did—although not right away. It took me a long time to be able to think about each one of those boys and then pray for God to bless him. But when I was able to do it, I really meant it!"

Forgiveness was beautiful for Mary Ann. She looked like a different person—her eyes were no longer shaded with sadness. We talked as we had never talked before—openly, honestly, sharing our deepest, most vulnerable feelings. Mary Ann was no longer afraid of people or of life. She was healed.

I don't know what will happen with Mary Ann and Hal—they are seeing each other again, and Hal still wants Mary Ann to marry him. Perhaps, in time . . .

Above all else, God is love. He also is holy. In his love he has marked out a plan that enables us—the sinners, the alienated, the lonely—to have a real relationship with him who is holy. He has offered us Christ, "who his own self bore our sins in his body on the tree."

What a generous plan! But what a price God had to pay.

We ourselves never could have repaid our debt to God—it was too big. We had refused to live his way, we had turned our back upon his love. Such a debt only God himself could pay. . . . On the cross "God was in Christ personally reconciling the world to himself" (II Corinthians 5:19, Phillips). It was a simple—and magnificent—act in which "God tasted death for every man" (Hebrews 2:9).

It is hard for us to understand exactly what God did in sending Jesus, his son, to live and die for us, but I suspect that as we grow in our understanding, we will be less likely to take our sin lightly, realizing how much forgiveness has cost God. We would certainly be less likely to say—as some did to Paul—"Let us sin that grace may abound."

Yes—when we ask it of him, God forgives us totally. He loves us that much . . . but that doesn't mean sin is irrelevant. God is not a sentimental father who delights in indulging his pampered children. When we turn our backs on his generosity, he, as a holy God of love, cannot overlook our sin. When we don't take his holiness seriously, we run the risk of diminishing the gospel to what Richard Neibuhr, the church historian, describes as "a God without wrath brought men without judgment through the ministry of a Christ without a Cross."

As James Devy put it, "To take the condemnation out of the Cross is to take the nerve out of the Gospel."

Forgiveness—free? Yes! Cheap—never! It is as cheap as God's Son.

I was a little girl during World War II, but I remember those stars in the windows of families whose sons or daughters had died in the fighting. Our friend, the Reverend Herb Meza, expressing it symbolically, says, "God has a star in his window—a star for a Son who died so that all men might be free to live in loving relationship with him. I wonder if that could have been what lit the skies that first Christmas season?"

I am an incurable clipper. Whenever I read anything that offers some insight into my relationship with God, I cut it out or copy it down and file it away. (And I have friends who share their treasures with me.) Unfortunately, in my eagerness to store away the information before it gets lost, I often neglect to write down the source of the article. I was guilty of such an oversight with a clipping I found in my files, one which is too penetrating to pass up. I honestly do not know where this comment comes from, but if I ever find out I will thank the author personally and everlastingly, for in this simple description he or she has captured the essence of Christ's meaning in our lives:

"It had been snowing for twenty-four hours. Knowing that it had been a hard winter, I filled the bird feeder with an extra supply of feed that morning. Since the feeder was sheltered, it held the only food not hidden by the snow. A short while later a small bird appeared in the yard, obviously weak, hungry, and cold. Searching for food, he pecked at the snow. How helpless I felt! I wanted to go out and point to the feeder; but if I had opened the door to throw out more food, he would have flown away.

"Then I realized that only if I were another bird could I indicate to him where he could find food. Only if I were another bird could I fly with him, identify myself with his hunger and cold, and let him know that I understood and cared.

"Our God, looking at man, knew that he must become one of us in order that we might understand his language; in order that we might know his love; in order that we might know his forgiveness; in order that we might point above our heads to the source of nourishment and eternal life."

James Buswell, Jr., said, "No one ever really forgives another—except he bears the penalty of the other's sin against him." Jesus on the cross is the perfect example of that kind of substitution. God loves us *that much!*

You say you feel unworthy? Join the crowd!

You long, with all your heart, to be a better person? Remember—God accepts you . . . right now . . . exactly as you are. And if you accept him as he is, the miracle will happen. You and he—together—will be able to do something about what you would like to be!

III

THE GIVE-AND-TAKE
OF FORGIVING

_C⁄◯_ One of the great joys in life comes from watching a troubled person turn and go in a new—and better—direction. What causes such a thing to happen? A miracle? Sometimes. Forgiveness? Always!

Tom was a charming child, as most rascals are—but he was rebellious, a prankster, a rule breaker, a flaunter of authority. By the time he entered high school, his reputation had preceded him and he filled most of the teachers with dread. He took a special delight in disrupting classes and driving teachers to the limits of their patience. At home, he also was a problem. There were frequent confrontations between parents and child, each one seeking to prove he was more powerful than the other.

So many complaints were filed against Tom that the high school principal decided he would have to expel him—unless a teacher named Mrs. Warren agreed to take him into her class. Mrs. Warren was an exceptionally capable English teacher, but she also was a loving, endlessly patient woman who seemed to have a way with problem students. Yes, Mrs.

Warren said, she would find a place for him in her eleven o'clock English Literature class, and also in her home room. She listened calmly as the principal read from a list of Tom's misdemeanors—a long list that had the principal shaking his head as he read. No, Mrs. Warren said, she wouldn't change her mind. She knew what she was getting into—she had heard about the boy.

When Tom was transferred to Mrs. Warren's class he behaved as he always did upon meeting a new teacher. He slouched in his seat in the last row and glared at her, daring her—by his attitude—to do something about him. At first Mrs. Warren ignored him. Then, as the class began to discuss the reading assignment, Tom whispered a joke to the boy in front of him, making the boy laugh. Mrs. Warren looked up. Then she closed her book, stood and placed another chair at the desk, next to hers.

"Tom, come up here and sit with me for a while," she said —not as a reprimand, but as a friend. It was an invitation she was offering, and her manner was so sweet that Tom couldn't refuse. He sat next to her as she went on with the lesson. "Tom is new to our class and hasn't had time to read the assignment, so if you'll bear with me, I'll read it aloud to him."

With Tom next to her, sharing her book, Mrs. Warren began to read from *A Tale of Two Cities*. She was a fine reader and captured Dickens' sense of drama magnificently. Tom, for all his determination to be an obstruction, found himself following the text, losing himself in the unfolding of a great story, sharing the excitement of it with a woman who really seemed to care about his interest in the book. That evening he startled his parents by sitting down—

without any prodding—to do his homework—at least the assignment for Mrs. Warren's class.

That was only the beginning. . . . Tom never missed a day of school after that first day in Mrs. Warren's class. Sometimes he cut other classes but never hers. He sat in the front row, participated in discussions, and seemed to enjoy reading aloud when he was called upon to do so. His appetite for reading suddenly became ravenous, and he asked Mrs. Warren to make up a list of books she thought he might enjoy in his free time. After school he stayed in the classroom when the other students went home and had long talks with Mrs. Warren about the things he had read and the ideas they stimulated.

Tom wasn't exactly an angel in other classes, but the effect of his behavior in Mrs. Warren's class began to rub off a little—for which the other teachers were most grateful.

Tom didn't finish high school. In his junior year, after an angry outburst at home, he defiantly joined the Navy. He didn't even say good-by to Mrs. Warren, who was very sad to see him leave school, because she thought she had failed in her attempt to reach him.

Seven years later, when Mrs. Warren was closing up her desk one afternoon before leaving for home, a young man came to the doorway and stood there, smiling. He was much taller and more muscular now, but Mrs. Warren recognized him within seconds. It was Tom! He rushed to her and hugged her so hard her glasses slid down her nose.

"Where have you been?" she said, adjusting her glasses and looking at him intently. My—he was so clear-eyed, so happy and self-confident!

"In school," he said, laughing.

"But I thought—"

"Sure, you thought I was in the Navy. . . . Well, I was, for a while. I went to school there."

It was a long story he had to tell. Thanks to the Navy he was able to finish high school . . . and then he went on to college courses. When his enlistment was up he got a job and continued his education at night. During that time he met a lovely girl. By the time he graduated he was married and had a son. Then he went on to graduate school, also at night.

"Well, what are you doing with your fine education?" Mrs. Warren asked.

"I'm a teacher—I teach English . . . especially to kids who disrupt other classes."

Tom had never forgotten the feeling of acceptance he had had from that first day in Mrs. Warren's class. More than all the threats, all the arguments and confrontations he had known, her forgiving love got through to him. And now he was passing that love on to other young people. He had learned the give-and-take of forgiveness.

Our son Jamie's buddies made him a banner for Christmas last year. It reads: "Love is a basket with five loaves and two fishes—it's never enough until you start to give it away." Forgiveness can work only if it flows from God to us and on to others. If we hold it to ourselves, refusing to pass it on, we destroy it. Until we ourselves have been forgiven by God, we cannot truly forgive others . . . but once we have accepted his divine pardon, we cannot refuse to give it away to others.

As someone said, "An unforgiving heart is unforgivable."

CHAPTER 7

When You Want to Be Forgiven

ℰℛ One of the hardest things in the world for us to do is forgive ourselves . . . and yet we must get beyond this obstacle if we are to know the peace that comes from complete forgiveness.

Perhaps the first step toward being forgiven is what keeps many of us from forgiving—this business of repentance. H-m-m . . . the very sound of the word conjures up images of fingers shaken in my face, scowls—Wait a moment! That's the Accuser at work again.

Let me try, instead, to deal with the word as God interprets it.

Repentance . . . In the Old Testament, *to repent* means to change one's moral direction. In the New Testament it means "to change one's purpose, or intent—to change one's mind." So repentance involves the way we live and the way we think.

Before we can turn away from sin, we must turn toward God. . . . Before we can honestly repent, we must admit our wrongs and confess them to God. We have to soul-search . . . and it takes courage to confront our inner life. We have to stop dipping our finger tips into the finger bowl and claiming we are clean all over.

In a very honest letter, a mother expresses the misgivings many parents feel somewhere deep inside themselves:

"Our failures—that's the hardest area, especially when they have affected the lives of our loved ones. As our two children step into the adult world, it is a joy to see many beautiful things in their lives. But it hurts to see areas of need and struggle that stem in part from ways we have failed them.

"A friend reminded me recently that even these areas are part of the 'all things' which God will use to make a man and woman who will accomplish his unique purposes. So when thoughts of my failures push their way into my consciousness, I let his total forgiveness dissolve my regrets, and go on to praise him who accepts us all just as we are and lovingly works to make us more than we are.

"He doesn't expect us—or our children—to be finished products now."

Children have to forgive their parents so many things that sometimes it makes one tremble at the thought of being a parent. But we are *not* perfect . . . neither must we and our children expect perfection of each other.

In my own moments of doubt, I have been helped by a prayer spoken by another mother. . . . "Lord Jesus, fill the gap between the love I have given my children and the love they need. Amen" (Ruth Stapleton, *The Gift of Inner Healing*, Word Books).

There simply is no way around confession. We cannot receive all that God has promised as long as we harbor resentment, pride, or ugly thoughts against others.

Confession, therefore, is amazingly practical—it is the act of spelling out our sin so that God can deal with it. Absolution—the release from our wrongdoings—is his work.

When we confess, we do more than admit our faults, we drop our defenses and come to grips with our inner selves, we stop blaming life, our parents, our friends, or the "breaks" for our uneasiness. We take the blame ourselves.

Some people think they can leave sin alone and let "time take care of it." Time may heal sorrow but it doesn't eradicate sin. Neglect will not do, for sin cries out for attention . . . and if we do not allow God to overcome it, it will overcome us.

Some shy away from confession, thinking it is a morbid preoccupation with sin. That's a misunderstanding, because confession is our way of getting rid of sin, not dwelling on it. I really enjoy cleaning my house—not because I take a morbid delight in dirt, but because I *like* a clean house.

Sometimes it helps to confess to another person after one has confessed to God . . . I don't know why this is so, but talking about our sins to an objective listener can help us gain some perspective on what we have done. Of course, it depends upon the person, the listener, and the sin. . . .

Dr. Lee Travis, our dear friend and Dean Emeritus of the Graduate School of Psychology, Fuller Theological Seminary, explains how "the productions of therapy are really confessions. . . .

"The patient speaks in metaphor, parable, innuendo, dreams of the day and of the night, fantasies, and picture language. He tries to say what is not openly said. . . . He wants to reveal, but fears to do so. As the therapist accepts what his patient is able to say and lets him know that he also accepts the deeper significance beneath his statements, the therapist is really forgiving the patient and is helping him forgive himself.

"By forgiving another, we clear the way for him to forgive himself. But first it is well to learn what it is that we and he should forgive. Therapy learns the answer to his question. The therapist withdraws completely as the judge, as a public prosecutor, and becomes a public defender of the patient's right to be whole. The patient must get the past confessed and forgiven. He must travel in the deep paths of his unconscious. He must come to know the long-dead characters in his past in order that he may hold them up to the light of this present day. Undigested feelings lying buried in yesterday's rubble need to be put in proper relation to the patient's current claim of accountability. His own right to judge himself must be valid in including all of himself in the judgment."

How many of us, having received God's pardon, are still unable to pardon ourselves? Perhaps we are all too aware that we—and others like us—fall far short of God's unending mercy. *Yes,* we tell ourselves, *Jesus understands . . . but will other people?* Conscious of our deficiencies, we usually are too hard on ourselves.

When I was an actress, I had an agent, a very dear man and a good friend. After I left my career—for the one I wanted more—Mel and I continued to be friends, and it was always a treat for us to get together with him and his beautiful wife, Rosita. On one occasion, I decided to make it a very special evening because we hadn't seen Mel and Rosita for a long time. I spent the entire day in the kitchen—something I rarely do but truly enjoy—preparing a gourmet meal. Then I set a beautiful table and lit the candles in the candelabra. Louie started a fire in the fireplace. Everything was lovely . . . except that our guests never arrived.

After an hour, we became concerned. Had something happened to Mel and his wife? Did their car break down somewhere? We called their home, and Mel answered the phone. He had completely forgotten about our dinner date!

Poor Mel! He was devastated with embarrassment and regret. In fact, he felt so bad that Louie and I wanted to do something to make him feel better. Sure, we were disappointed, we told him—but it was only a dinner . . . and, after all, Louie and I had so little time to ourselves that we would enjoy the evening anyway. . . . But nothing we could say eased Mel's discomfort. The next day he sent flowers—a huge bouquet of roses—and the day after that we got a letter from him. It was filled with abject apologies and self-blame. That night he called again to tell us how sorry he was—and finally Louie had to interrupt him, saying, "Hey, Mel, stop it! We love you! Now, you didn't hurt anybody, so stop feeling guilty." At last Mel understood. We made another dinner date and had a lovely time together.

The truth is, we cannot even forgive ourselves—by ourselves. We are so ready to blame ourselves that we often feel guilty when we haven't even done anything wrong. . . . We are like the people who automatically feel responsible for anything that goes wrong—someone once called them "blame-blotters." Here, too, our imperfect humanity gets in our way, and so, again, we must go to God.

Self-blame is like an infection that spreads to all parts of our lives, weakening the healthy areas. . . .

I met Denise during a church family retreat. She had worked hard all her life, had helped put her husband through medical school and at the same time took wonderful care of their four children. Understandably she was tired —but more than that, she was being eaten away by feelings of guilt that went far back in her life.

When Denise was a child, she knew that her parents loved her, but she longed to see their love demonstrated, and it never was. Her mother was attentive but never cuddled her children, never kissed them. As Denise grew up, she and her mother clashed often. It wasn't that they disliked each other . . . they just seemed to antagonize each other. After Denise was married, she moved away from the town where she was brought up and seldom saw her mother. But, as before, when they were together, they argued and disagreed over the slightest thing.

As the years went by, Denise began to feel guilty because she had never told her mother how much she loved her. "I just couldn't bring myself to do it—I don't know why," she said. "And yet I loved my mother very much. I knew she wanted me to tell her, but she wouldn't come right out and ask me. She was too stubborn—and so was I."

Denise's husband became a doctor, and as his practice grew, life became easier for them. Still, Denise was tired, easily upset, irritable—her marriage was hurt by her distress. She knew she was taking out her guilt feelings on her husband and her children, and hated herself for doing it, but she could not stop.

At the church family retreat, Denise was able to put her

feelings into words, and that helped a lot. But she needed more than any of her church friends could give her—she needed to get in touch with God. We urged her to pray—not formally, but spontaneously, as if she were talking to her best friend, which she was! We encouraged her to tell God what she had done and admit to him that she couldn't forgive herself. Would he do it for her?

He did more than that. . . . As Denise prayed, she began to look back over her childhood and see things she had overlooked when she was a little girl. Her mother had had a terrible fear that she was going to die at a young age, and because she thought she would be taken away from her children while they were still young, she dared not allow herself to hold them close to her. . . . It was too painful for her. Denise did not believe her mother had done the right thing, yet now she could understand why she behaved as she did. . . . Mother and daughter were still two entirely different personalities—perhaps they would never have a harmonious relationship, but they could acknowledge their love for each other.

One day Denise sat down and began to write a letter to her mother. She wrote for hours, pouring out her love for her mother and asking her forgiveness for never saying, "I love you." The moment she put the letter in the mailbox, she felt better than she had felt in months—years. She wasn't so tired any more . . . new energy seemed to pour into her life.

Two weeks later Denise's mother became very ill and died. But a friend who had been with her wrote Denise and told her how much Denise's letter had meant to her mother. She was too weak to write to Denise, but she read the letter over and over, and when she could no longer hold it up to the light, she asked her friend to read it to her. "Your mother died a happy woman," the friend told Denise.

Denise was able to right the wrong she had done—and just in time. For some of us it may be too late, and for others it may not be wise. One man, having confessed an adulterous relationship to God, felt no peace until he also confessed it to his wife. She was wonderfully able to forgive—in fact, she had resources within her which her husband never knew existed. Their story had a happy ending, but that is not always so. I have known of other instances where the admission of adultery was just too much for one of the partners to accept . . . it was a destructive, rather than a healing, force.

Confession to God is always necessary to a restoration of love, but telling another person that we have wronged him or her is a decision we have to weigh carefully. We have to ask ourselves: Will my confession be constructive in this relationship? Will it heal the hurt? Or will it become a barrier that nothing will be able to remove? So much depends upon the persons involved—their strengths, their faith, their ability to face a painful truth. I would hate to—in fact, I could not—say "This is what everyone should do" about confessing to another person.

Confession may be a release to you, but may place a terrible burden on the other person—perhaps one the person is not able to bear. Such healing—which involves another person's suffering—may not be a healing at all. The decision belongs to God. The guidance of the Holy Spirit is the most practical help I can suggest.

Once we have confessed to God—and perhaps to others— the give-and-take of forgiveness begins to work in our lives. We *should* feel relief . . . peace . . . renewed communication with God and with our fellow men—that is, *if* we are able to accept forgiveness. Some of us can't.

Some of us can't accept forgiveness because we just don't feel worthy of it. For many of us, this conviction that we are unlovable began in early childhood. If we were not beautiful . . . or strong . . . or brilliant . . . perhaps people didn't give us the strokes they reserve for the "beautiful" children. And if we were beautiful, we may have been "different" in some way . . . and with the same devastating results.

If that was so in your life, then your first step toward forgiveness is to believe you are worthy of it . . . not because of anything you have or have not done, but because of God's great mercy. You are worth it to him. God loves you! He created you . . . you are his child, and he desires a relationship with you. That means you are special . . . and somewhere close by you there are people who will know you are special. Find them . . . let God lead you to them . . . and put yourself in the way of a blessing.

CHAPTER 8

When You Want to Forgive

⟨⟩ Children can be cruel—we all know that. I learned it as a little girl, a child of divorced parents who was brought up by a mother and grandfather. How I loved the two wonderful adults in my life! Yet, in my early years, I was painfully aware of not having a father. Sometimes, at school events and social functions, I used to stand near the father of another child, hoping people would think he was *my* father. The worst time for me, though, was the day my little friends formed a circle around me and sang, as they danced to Ring-Around-the-Rosie: "Colleen doesn't have a daddy! Colleen doesn't have a daddy!"

Yes, that hurt . . . but I am older now and I can look back and realize that the children who did it simply didn't understand—sometimes cruel things are done without the intent to hurt, and it helps to know that. Understanding makes a difference in the way we look at life.

It takes two to work through forgiveness—God and us. Actually, it takes God working *in* us . . . and our willingness to work it *out* in life.

Even if we cannot understand why someone offended us
. . . even if there are basic differences in the way we think
. . . we can still *be* understanding. It's a matter of attitude.
We can recognize the other person as someone of worth—he
or she is someone God loves, someone for whom Christ died,
and therefore a person of value.

Until recently Belinda found it impossible to forgive her
father for the terrible shame he had brought to her life. She
was very young when it happened, and until that time she
had adored her father. They had been very close, and
Belinda felt a special responsibility to bring cheer to her father's eyes when he was sad. And he was often sad, for there
were many problems in the man's life. . . . One day, in a
moment of deep anguish, he forced his daughter into an in-
cestuous relationship, one that continued for the next few
years until Belinda was able to leave home. She married,
hastily and regrettably. Within a few years she was divorced
and living alone, assaulted this time by the memories of her
hatred for her father.

Belinda married again. Her husband is a patient, understanding man who has been very supportive to her. Gradually she felt she could trust people—life—again. The only obstacle to her happiness was her poor health . . . often
during the night she would wake up with a feeling that she
was choking. . . . Sitting up, gasping for air, she thought
she was going to die. The attacks came more frequently,
more severely, and her doctors could do little or nothing for
her. She had a form of asthma for which there seemed to be
no physical basis . . . medicines offered no relief.

"I knew what it was," she said, "and I knew I would either die or go insane if I couldn't do something about my

hatred for my father. . . . That's what was choking me to
death!"

It was painful for Belinda to look back on that early time
in her life, but with God's help, she did. "Jesus—*you* forgive
my father, and then show me how," she prayed.

Something happened as she began to remember. . . . She
saw her father, not as a scorned and hated person, but as a
man with burdens he was unable to carry—the death of his
mother when he was a very little boy . . . years of neglect
as the youngest child in a large family whose members had
no time to love him . . . the hope for joy in his own wife
and children, and the sudden crushing of that hope with the
loss of a job . . . the deprivation of unemployment over a
long period of time, and the blow to his self-esteem when
his wife became the family breadwinner . . . the degrada-
tion and self-contempt that must have been his when he
turned, in desperation, to what he felt was the one source of
happiness in those lonely days—his daughter . . . and the
continued confirmation of his worthlessness by his repeated
abuse of her. . . .

None of those memories changed the facts for Belinda.
The events in her life were the same as she remembered
them—except that she no longer hated the pitiful, despairing
man her father had become. She understood him, she forgave him, even though she could not alter what he had done
—and that understanding saved her life and her sanity. The
terrible nighttime attacks of choking began to subside and
finally stopped. . . . Belinda slept peacefully.

We don't have to approve of a person's behavior in order
to accept him as a valued human being. Remember, God's

love sees past the behavior to the man or woman. And if his love is in us, we will *want* to forgive.

Forgiveness was costly to God, and it will cost us, too, so we must not make light of it. One of the most dehumanizing experiences we can have is to go to someone—after praying and asking for courage, yet still trembling—and ask him for forgiveness, only to have him say, "Forget it—it didn't mean a thing."

If forgiveness is important to a brother or a sister, it should become important to us. If we say it doesn't matter, we may think we are polite—but we are trying to avoid the issue, and that is basically dishonest. Forgiveness faces the issue—it wants to clear the mind of its clutter of grudges.

The best time to forgive is *now* . . . quickly! . . . without hesitation . . . before the wound becomes infected. If years have already gone by, *now* is the time to let love have its way. This is the moment to do something about the grudge you hold.

Do something? How? What? One Sunday before communion, a minister made a suggestion to the congregation: "Think of the person who has hurt you the most," he said. "Forgive that person, and then go home and write or call him. *Do* something!"

A man named Jim said he felt as if his minister had singled him out—because for several years Jim had refused to forgive someone who had once been a close friend. After the communion service Jim went home and thought about his friend for a long time. The friend really had hurt him, had told a lie that damaged Jim's reputation. Later the friend was sorry for what he had done, but forgiveness was out of the question for Jim—until that Sunday morning in church.

"I decided to write to my friend, and I spent all afternoon writing letter after letter. But when I showed each version to my wife, she pointed out that I was writing to tell my friend how wrong he had been. I wasn't any closer to forgiving him."

Jim wrestled with forgiveness for a long time. He couldn't reach that point, yet he couldn't put it from his mind. He knew that his minister was right—he had to *do* something. Finally he realized what his minister was getting at—Jim had to take his grudge to God before he could do anything at all. He had to let God do something *for* him.

Jim prayed for the ability to forgive, and as he did he began to remember all the things he loved about his friend—his support, his sense of humor, his dependability, his concern. He had been a fine friend, except for that one moment of weakness. And then Jim discovered something very important.

"I've always been hard on myself," he said. "My standards of behavior are very high. So I guess I'm pretty hard on others, too. I wouldn't have been able to forgive myself if I had done what my friend did—and, of course, I couldn't forgive him either. I was too doggoned proud! Now I had two things to pray about—forgiving myself for my stubbornness and forgiving my friend."

With God's help, Jim was able to do both. The next time he wrote a letter to his friend, he spoke of love and friendship and forgiveness—and he mailed that letter! A week later he received a letter from his friend. Then there were phone calls and a visit—a reunion of two men in a friendship that promises to be deeper and more committed than ever before. And Jim? Forgiveness has changed Jim's life in other ways. His standards still are high, but they are flexible enough to deal with human failure.

"I think I began to live by my faith in Christ the day I asked God to teach me how to forgive a friend," he said.

Art Nelson, a respected, long-time member of our congregation, traveled many, many miles in order to forgive something that was done to him when he was a little boy. Art was only two years old when his mother died. After his father remarried and had children by his second wife, Art found himself unwanted, rejected, the victim of brutal outbursts of cruelty. For most of his early years he suffered in body and in spirit, but the one thing that kept him going was his feeling of kinship with God. "Sometimes he used to pick me up when I couldn't even walk, I was so hurt," he said. "I know it was God who did it, because no one else would have."

Finally, when Art was fifteen, he had a chance to live with a family who gave him the love he desperately needed. He vowed he would have nothing to do with his parents again. He thought he had forgiven them . . . in fact, he thought he forgave them at the very moment they were hurting him. But he didn't want to see them—not ever.

As the years passed, Art's parents, who lived in Sweden, wrote to him many times, asking him to forgive them for what they had done to him. But as far as he was concerned, he had already forgiven them, and so most of the time their letters went unanswered. They begged him to visit them in Sweden so that they could see him at least once before they died, but Art knew he would never go.

And then, one Christmas Eve, after having taken communion, Art and his wife, Millie, were driving home when Art suddenly began to think about his parents. He felt as if a voice were speaking in his ear, saying, "You have not done enough. You must go to them quickly."

"I felt possessed by guilt," he said. "I was afraid I would be too late."

Art and Millie made plans to go to Sweden immediately. Usually Millie doesn't like to fly, but she, too, felt the urgency of the moment and suggested they go by plane.

The reunion was so beautiful that Art gets tears in his eyes when he describes it. His father, wearing his best suit and a white cravat, and his stepmother, badly crippled by arthritis, met Art and Millie at the airport. The first words his stepmother said were, "Forgive me for what I have done to you" . . . and Art was so overcome with an awareness of God's love flowing through him that he took her in his arms and said, "And *you* forgive *me* for those times when I wasn't a good boy."

It was a lovely visit, and a few weeks later Art and his wife left for home. This time they went by boat. By the time they got home there were letters waiting for them. Two were from Art's half brother in Sweden. One informed Art that his stepmother had died the day he left Sweden. The other letter said that Art's father had died a few days later. "They lived only to see you once more, and they both died in peace," the second letter read.

For Art Nelson, the act of forgiving was complete . . . and just in time!

Now, we all don't have to write letters or cover long distances in order to forgive. But sometimes—many times, for me—it does help to do *something*, to perform some act or gesture that cancels out the hurt as tangibly as if we had marked a big X through it.

I find that communion is a wonderful means of grace . . . somehow, taking the bread and the wine when I have something to forgive seems to settle the matter. And so, if our church isn't serving communion when I am working out a forgiveness, I find a church that is. I go there to worship, perhaps anonymously, but in the presence of brothers and sisters in Christ, appropriating that real means of grace into my life.

When you want to forgive, don't "try harder." That is not what God tells us to do. God himself wants to do something —*has* done something—which we can never do for ourselves.

When you want to forgive, let God do it for you. Just say, "Help me, Jesus"!

In the novel *The Mansion*, Gertrude Atherton tells the story of an unfaithful husband who finally confesses his infidelity to his wife. His wife, her eyes wet with tears, turns to him and says, "I do not see yet how it will be best to do it, but—you and I must work this out together." What an affirmation—a reaffirmation—of a wonderful relationship in which love had the final word!

Within a family, forgiveness is a necessary part of the daily relationship. It opens the way to real, rather than conditional, loving.

It has been said that "because we love them so much, no one can hurt us quite as much as our children," but children also have to forgive their parents. No matter how hard we may try not to, we parents do leave our imprints in the soft clay of our children's lives. . . . We are marred and scarred by each other. The solution is not perfection, but for-giveness. Children, at some point, have to realize that their parents also had parents who shaped them. We all need God to heal and reshape our lives. To function fully as an adult, each of us has the choice of carrying the hurt child for the rest of our lives—or forgiving each other our imperfections.

Forgiveness can bring a family closer together. . . . It has happened in our family many times. And I shall never forget the beauty of one of those experiences, when our oldest son, Danny, was just a little fellow, about six years old. He had always been co-operative, never difficult, until—one day Louie visited Danny's Sunday school class. He came as minister, not as father, and he was shocked to find his son disrupting the class with his antics. The teacher was barely able to control the class, and Louie was barely able to con-trol his temper. He had never seen Danny like that before!

It was a serious little boy and a serious father who faced each other at home later after church. Louie left no doubt in anyone's mind that he was going to apply some "discipline," but first, in fairness, he thought he ought to give Danny a chance to explain what happened.

The two of them marched off to a bedroom where they could be alone. "Okay, son," Louie began, "do you realize that you gave your teacher a very hard time this morning?"

Danny stared at the floor. "Yes," he muttered.

"And do you realize you spoiled the lesson for the other children?"

Another mutter. "Yes."

"Well, do you think that was a good thing for you to do?"

The little head shook from side to side slowly, the eyes still staring at the floor.

"Then why did you do it, son?"

Danny raised his head, his clear blue eyes meeting Louie's. "Daddy, you've been too busy lately," he said.

Louie was stunned. "What?"

"You've broken your promise to keep our family time—you're away too much."

All Louie's anger left him and he knelt down to speak to Danny, eyeball to eyeball. He *had* been very busy—for several weeks. Each week he was supposed to spend one day with the children and me—away from his work—and lately he had been putting us off, promising to make up the time later. He meant those promises, we all knew that, but there never seemed to be any "later."

"Danny," he said, "I'm very sorry I haven't been with you as much as we both wanted. I'll try not to let myself get that busy ever again—I promise you. Will you forgive me, Danny, for being too busy now?"

Danny's eyes were filled with tears. "Sure," he said. "Will you forgive me for what *I* did today?"

"Of course!" Louie said, throwing his arms around Danny. The two of them clung to each other, and then they got down on their knees and prayed together. I'm not sure what else took place, but when they joined the rest of us for lunch they were red-eyed, arm in arm, and definitely launched into a new relationship.

Between a husband and wife, how important it is to forgive. Much as we may love to guard our grudges and hug our hurts, a forgiving life-style means we must give up these dubious pleasures.

Real love in a marriage brings two persons so close that the possibility of joy and pain is ever-present. I can tell in an instant—from just a glance—if I have hurt Louie, or if I have been careless of love. At such a time the two most healing words I can say are, "I'm sorry!"

"I'm sorry" . . . they are more than words. . . . They are hands reaching out across the distance between us and another . . . re-establishing the relationship, and offering the other person the mercy that he or she in turn will pass on to others. Unless we take this final step—unless the relationship is continued and strengthened with the bonds of genuine love, we have not experienced complete forgiveness.

Sometimes, though—we tell ourselves—this is not possible. We may forgive but we can't forget—and the remembering gets in the way of the relationship. A couple who are friends of ours tell me that when they keep going over and over something they think they have forgiven, that's when they can be sure they really *haven't* forgiven.

"Forgive and forget" is easy to say but not always possible to do. . . . In fact, it may not be the best thing for us to do when we have been hurt. We can't forgive someone by trying to forget what he or she has done—and the more we try to forget, the more we are likely to remember. Our memories may be healed in time—forgetting may be a final, eventual step in the process of forgiveness, but if it is, it comes to us through God's grace and not our own efforts, however well intended they may be.

Sometimes I *do* forget after forgiving . . . and sometimes the memory remains—but it no longer hurts, and the absence of pain can make a continued relationship possible.

Clara Barton, the inspiration and organizer of the American Red Cross, made some enemies in the course of her long career. She was outspoken, sometimes impatient in her eagerness for justice and mercy. Sometimes her enemies lashed out at her work and attacked her reputation. When she was asked about one particular critic who had treated her most unjustly, she replied, "I distinctly remember forgetting that."

I came across a prayer written by Ruth Stapleton (*The Gift of Inner Healing*, Word Books) a woman who has a deep understanding of the need for healing our memories. This prayer may not touch you at all where you live—on the other hand, it may have the same profound significance for you that it has had for me:

"My earthly father—I forgive you for not being there when I needed you. . . . I forgive you for the things Mother and I needed which you never provided. . . . I forgive you, and I see that you could not be all those things at that time.

"If I have ever hurt you in any way, please forgive me. In his name. Amen."

CHAPTER 9

Love Doesn't Always Win

℮℩℈ At 4 A.M. I was still tossing and turning. . . . I was angry with her for not letting me try to heal our wounded relationship. How was I to deal with such a person?

For some time I had been aware of the need for healing between us. . . . In fact, ever since she had known me she had been against me—I never knew why. I knew I had done *something*—or hadn't done something—but I didn't know what. Everything I did or thought or said seemed to rub her the wrong way. I felt terrible about it. I tried so hard to make her my friend because I truly wanted to be *her* friend. She was a young widow, a dynamic woman. I admired her, respected her, really liked her—but the feeling wasn't mutual. Friends who knew us both alluded to her negative feelings about me . . . and when we were together in a group there were little digs.

And then, at one point in my journey with Christ, I had a deep experience with the Holy Spirit that left me filled with an overwhelming sense of love—especially for this person from whom I felt such rejection. I felt led to go and see her so that I could talk these things out with her. I wanted to tell her, face to face, how much I wanted her friendship . . . and that there was only love in my heart for her. So I called her up and then I drove to her home in a neighboring city where she and her children had moved.

My heart was pounding in my throat as I began to tell her that I was aware of her attitude toward me. I recalled some of the hurtful remarks that had come back to me from others—and the jibes and digs I had heard and had been unable to forget. It felt so good to talk about them, to get them out into the open. That moment was very important to me. . . . I was excited at the prospect of being reconciled.

She heard me out. Then, looking puzzled, she shook her head. "I really don't know what you're talking about," she said. "You and I have never been at odds. I have, in fact, the greatest respect for you and your husband."

The pounding of my heart got louder. I couldn't believe what I was hearing. . . .

"As far as I know," she went on, "there is nothing for us to discuss."

Talk about having egg on your face! I felt sick. My approach had been rejected. . . . Thanks, but no thanks. And yet, I had felt so *led* to go to her. Surely the Holy Spirit knew what he was doing! Or had I misinterpreted him somewhere along the way?

I kept asking myself all those questions—over and over—until the wee hours of the morning. It was then I heard the voice that was not a voice saying, "Whether she accepts your attempt at reconciliation is not your responsibility. . . . Forgive her for *not* forgiving." And with God's help, that is what I did. Only then did I sleep.

When I awoke later that morning I was tired—but free! No longer did I feel compelled to please this woman or go out of my way to prove I was worthy of her friendship. I loved her—she didn't have to feel the same way. Love doesn't always win, but being able to love is what counts.

A woman who was appointed president of a large department store had a similar experience. Irene is an extremely capable administrator, well qualified for such an important position, but she was the first woman to have the job and understandably she was a little nervous during those first few days. The store was in trouble—sales had fallen off and profits were down—Irene had been promoted in the hope that she might bring some new creative approach to the store's methods of merchandising.

Irene already thought she knew why the store was in trouble. Its merchandise had not kept up with the needs and tastes of young working people who make up a large segment of the buying public. Irene wanted to encourage the store's buyers to try new products, so she instituted a weekly series of meetings with all the merchandising personnel. Everyone was encouraged to suggest ways in which the store could take on a new image with the public and thereby excite more interest among its customers.

Most of the buyers were enthusiastic about changing the merchandise, but a few resented the idea. One woman, in particular, who had been with the store for as long as anyone could remember, voiced her objection in no uncertain terms one day after Irene left the meeting. She criticized

Irene personally and said she wished she would stop "wasting everyone's time with these silly pep talks."

When Irene heard about the remark she was furious. She knew she had to do something immediately or her position of authority would be shaken. So she called the woman to her office and told her that, while she had no objection to criticism, such remarks made in her absence, and in public, must stop.

The buyer was terribly upset. "Well, if that's the way I am to be treated here—after so many years—I think I ought to quit!"

Irene tried to reason with the woman but only seemed to increase her distress. What would the woman do without her job? She was experienced and talented, but she was almost sixty-five years old, too near the age of retirement to get a job anywhere else.

For days Irene was troubled by the scene in her office. She knew she had done the right thing. She had not abused her authority. But she didn't want the buyer to resign and she felt personally responsible for her.

One evening on her way home from her office, Irene approached a church and felt the urge to go inside and pray. The door was open and no one was inside. She sat down and let her whole body relax as she gave her anxiety and concern to God. "What shall I do, Lord?" she asked.

The answer was unexpected.

"I was told—quite unmistakably—to forgive the woman and to apologize for causing her anxiety. I had done nothing wrong in speaking to her as I did. I had stood on my rights. But now God was asking me not to stand on them any longer. I had hurt the woman's feelings. She needed my comfort, not my authority."

On the way to the office the next morning Irene passed a flower vendor. Impulsively she bought a bunch of daffodils and took them to the buyer's office, but as she held them out the woman said, "I don't like flowers."

"Then may I say something?" Irene asked. Without waiting for a reply, she went on. "Can't we forget what happened the other day? It was such a trivial matter. I've forgiven you for your remarks and I know it won't happen again. . . . Will you forgive me for upsetting you?"

"Well," said the woman, "it's a good thing you came to apologize, because otherwise I would have quit!" Not a word about forgiveness . . . accepted or given.

But Irene was free. Another buyer said, "I don't think the woman understands what you have done. How on earth *did* you do it?"

Irene smiled and put the daffodils in a vase on her desk. "I didn't," she said. "God did."

Later she wrote to me: "God sometimes asks us to do the illogical thing, to give up our authority, our self-righteous position, to humble ourselves and do his will. The amazing thing is the great joy and peace that come from such an act!"

No, love doesn't always win. . . . Neither does it lose. Christ, by his example, tells us to forgive even those who have not admitted and confessed their wrongdoing . . . even when they are not yet aware that they have hurt or wounded . . . even when they do not know he said, "Father, forgive them, for they know not what they do."

Beyond forgetting and leaving the hurt behind us, we can

do something to heal the wound. Sometimes this works, sometimes it doesn't. . . . Success is not guaranteed. But, remember—even Jesus did not win them all. . . .

Try . . . take the risk . . . in the doing there is freedom!

CHAPTER 10

How Often Should You Forgive?

℮ℓ⌀ "Then Peter approached him with the question, 'Master, how many times can my brother wrong me and I must forgive him? Would seven times be enough?'

"'No,' replied Jesus, 'not seven times, but seventy times seven!'" (Matthew 18:21–22, Phillips).

Forgiveness is not a formula, but an attitude. If there were a limit to the number of times we should forgive—if, for instance 490 times were sufficient—then when a person was offended for the 491st time he could say, "That's it! I've done my part—no more forgiving required!" And all the other 490 times he had forgiven would have meant nothing at all, because he would not have acted in the true spirit of love.

Jesus tells us that seventy times seven is *not* 490. . . . Rather, it is innumerableness, indefiniteness, endlessness. There is no way to measure it. He says it does not matter how many times we are called upon to forgive . . . we must do it every time.

Under the rabbinical law of Jesus' day, forgiveness was required three times and no more. So perhaps Peter thought he was very generous in more than doubling the number of times an offense might be repeated and still be forgiven. And so he asks: "Master, how many times can my brother wrong me and I must forgive him? Would seven times be enough?"

Had the brothers and sisters been trying Peter's patience? Were they mistreating him? Was he getting weary of forgiving and looking for a way out? At any rate, the question was not unnatural. But it was founded on a misconception which Jesus dispelled with his reply. Peter's misconception—and it is ours, as well—is that we have a right to resent injury and hurt, that there is a limit to what we can take. Humanly speaking, this is true, but Jesus makes it clear that for his followers there is a radical new life-style in which the obligation to forgive is unlimited and unconditional.

The world of Jesus' day lived the law of retaliation, which required that the wrongdoers should "get what he gave." Jesus turned that law upside down when he said, "You have heard that it used to be said '*An eye for an eye and a tooth for a tooth,*' but I tell you, don't resist the man who wants to harm you. If a man hits your right cheek, turn the other one to him as well. If a man wants to sue you for your coat, let him have it and your overcoat as well. If anybody forces you to go a mile with him, do more—go two miles with him" (Matthew 5:38–42, Phillips).

For the followers of Christ there shall be no getting even. When evil is done to us, we do not repay in kind. This does not mean we are spineless, nor do we allow others to walk

all over us. To do so in the name of love would not be loving
—it benefits neither the oppressed nor the oppressor.

As Jesus' people we have access to the unlimited love and
forgiveness of God—it is not our own small supply of love
we are to use, for that would surely run out quickly. By accepting God's free gift of love, we are obligated to give the
same love to others. This is God's condition for forgiveness.

Here, though, we become acutely aware of our humanity.
We *do* have limits. We cannot be hurt again and again, and
still go on offering the other cheek. We want to do it—but
we just can't. We are not door mats! But then, neither was
Jesus Christ. . . . There were times when he denounced the
sin while loving the sinner—and we are to do the same.

We can love a person who is sick without condoning his
sick behavior. We can forgive the person who hurts us without excusing the hurt itself. . . . And here is where we must
draw the line.

During the early days of my husband's ministry I was really annoyed by the behavior of a member of the congregation. He was an older man named Howard, who had fond
memories of the minister he had known during his childhood and early youth. He idolized the man, who was now
deceased, and compared every minister—including my husband—to him. No matter what Louie did or how he did it,
Howard always had something to say about the way his
friend might have handled the same thing.

Now, I hate feeling defensive—but I felt *so* defensive
every time I was around Howard. Of course I also felt guilty
about it and kept trying to reach a point of forgiveness. At
the same time I was participating in a small group where we
were trying to learn how to express our real feelings instead

of holding them back until they exploded. Obviously I was on a collision course with some of my feelings because in my attempt to reach forgiveness I was repressing some honest reactions.

Well . . . one night at a meeting which Howard and I attended, Howard again began to criticize Louie and the other ministers on the staff, describing to everyone how he thought his childhood minister would have handled a similar situation. . . . And I could take it no longer. I realized that I was not loving Howard by just sitting there—silently—as he made his attacks on people. In other words, loving Howard was one thing . . . putting up with his negative behavior was another!

"Just a minute, Howard," I said, interrupting him. "There's something I've been wanting to say to you for a long time, and if I let it go any longer it's going to come out in a way neither of us will appreciate."

You could have heard a pin drop in the room—and a lot of people were present. Howard was astonished—and silent.

"I don't think any minister will ever please you," I said, "because he isn't the minister you loved as a child. Now, I'm sure that man was a fine minister in his way, just as I feel Louie and our other ministers are in theirs—but they are not the same. That's something I hope you'll be able to accept."

I felt so good! . . . And at last I could come to the point of forgiving Howard because that didn't mean I had to encourage his supercritical behavior. A few days later, Howard's wife said to me, "I don't know what went on at the meeting the other night, but whatever it was, it gave Howard an awful lot of respect for you."

"It gave me respect for him, too," I said. And it was

true. . . . Howard and I did learn to respect each other. In fact, we became good friends . . . and I couldn't help thinking that perhaps he always wanted people to tell him how they felt about his critical attitude. Anyway, he seemed pleased when someone did. Of course, it might not have had this happy ending. Howard might have been very miffed—but that is a risk we have to take if we are going to "speak the truth in love" to people.

Yes, we *are* called upon to forgive as many times as we are offended—but forgive what? If we say, "Oh, that's all right, go ahead and hurt me again," we are encouraging the person to continue the hurting. If we say, "I love you as a person, as a child of God—but I cannot let you do this to me," then we are distinguishing between the person and the action. We are letting the person know that we will continue our relationship with him, but we do not approve of the things he does. And this is our right. Turning the other cheek means that we are willing to be hurt again—and we do this by continuing the relationship. It does not mean we are willing to allow someone to walk all over us.

I don't hate someone who has a problem—*unless* I'm letting that problem manipulate me. If I am free to denounce the problem and still love the person, then I will have no reason to hate.

I have a friend whose mother is an alcoholic. For years my friend struggled with her feelings toward her mother, who, when she was drinking, was abusive and argumentative. It was impossible for her to talk to her mother without becoming angry, so my friend saw her as little as possible. She kept in touch by telephone and by writing letters.

One Easter Sunday my friend called her mother, and, as

usual, her mother began to quarrel with her. "God, help me deal with this," my friend prayed, and as she spoke the words, a feeling of peace came over her.

"I felt an immense love for my mother—I could distinguish between her and the effects of the drinks on the tormented woman at the other end of the line. Still, she was shouting at me, and I knew that if I continued to try to talk to her, I, too, would begin shouting. So I waited until she paused for a second and then I said, 'Mother, I love you very much, but I can't talk to you when you're this way. You're shouting so loud I can't hold the phone up to my ear. I'm going to hang up now, Mother, and then I'm going to call you back tomorrow when you feel better.'

"I hung up as gently as I could and did not answer the phone when it rang again later. I waited until the next day, and then I called my mother again. She was sober, and we had a decent conversation for the first time in years."

Only when my friend was able to see past the acts to the person committing them was she able to forgive . . . and love . . . and continue in the relationship. Now she knows how to forgive "seventy times seven."

IV

WALKING FREE

℘ Suzanne admits that she was a perfectionist and made life very hard for herself. But she also had to cope with some difficult circumstances.

Her husband's career was associated with politics and he was away from home frequently, often for long periods of time. When they were married, Suzanne accepted the necessity for Kurt's absences, but she was unprepared for the amount of work she would have to do—alone and unassisted —by the time they had three little children. Suzanne was a meticulous housekeeper—the kind who cannot bear to see a speck of dust on a tabletop or in a corner. She also was a conscientious and loving mother. In the early years of their marriage, Kurt's mother lived with them, part of the time as an invalid confined to her bed, and Suzanne was her devoted nurse.

Looking back, Suzanne realizes that part of the problem lay in the way she and Kurt had been brought up. In both their families, the women took care of the home and children and the men took care of business . . . so, no matter how overburdened Suzanne was, it never occurred to her to ask Kurt for help and it never occurred to him to offer it.

Suzanne was a healthy woman, but in time her energy became exhausted and the tasks she used to perform so cheerfully now wore her out. She felt guilty about her fatigue—in her eyes she was a failure as a mother, a wife, and a daughter-in-law. She was ashamed at the way she lost her temper under the slightest provocation, snapping at the children and bickering with Kurt.

As the bickering got worse, Suzanne and Kurt decided to see a marriage counselor recommended by their minister. Suzanne really didn't want to go, but she knew she had to do something about her way of life, so she bit her lip and kept the appointment.

The marriage counselor, who also was a minister, was very kind, very understanding. Suzanne had expected him to point the finger of blame at her, but instead he was sympathetic to her pain. He asked her and Kurt to tell him about some of the things that troubled them the most. As Suzanne began to describe her feelings of guilt about her inability to keep up with her work, something amazing happened to her. She could still hear the marriage counselor asking her questions—and she could hear herself answer—but part of her seemed to be somewhere else. A beautiful clear white light seemed to surround her, and she distinctly heard a voice telling her she was forgiven. . . . She was not to feel guilty any more. . . . She was loved by God and was his child. . . . And she was to give this love to those who had hurt her.

Suzanne was so overcome with relief that she could not say a word. At the end of the meeting she thanked the counselor and returned home with her husband. The next day she called the counselor and told him what had happened. He understood and was very happy for her.

"My life changed completely," Suzanne says. "I didn't suddenly wake up and feel energetic—no, it wasn't that simple. But I began to discover ways to take better care of my health. For instance, one day I was passing by a bookstore when I felt a sudden urge to go inside. When I did, and as I looked at shelf after shelf filled with books of all kinds, one book seemed to shout for my attention. It was a book about nutrition. I bought it and read it. I learned that I could increase my energy with a properly balanced diet—at least it was worth a try."

Suzanne is now an expert on nutrition and she enjoys glowing good health. . . . I wish I could do half the things she does without feeling tired.

Realizing that she was loved just the way she was, Suzanne became a much more relaxed person. She didn't have to be perfect—nor did her house. It was neat and comfortable, and that was enough.

Altering their roles as husband and wife was hard for Kurt and Suzanne. Helping Suzanne in the house did not come naturally to Kurt, and Suzanne often had to remind him to do something for her. She didn't relish that part of their readjustment, but neither did she feel guilty about it. She understood that she was not a failure and she was not doing anything wrong by living in a style that was different from the style of her parents.

Forgiveness went a long way with Suzanne—and so it should with each of us. If we accept the love that God so generously offers us, it can be the beginning of a new—and wonderfully free—way of life.

CHAPTER 11

In Touch with Life

e∕∽ When a little boy was asked to describe Jesus, he thought for a moment and then replied, "Jesus was the best picture God ever had taken."

Simple as it may appear, there is a lot of truth in his answer. If we want to see God, we should look at Jesus. . . . And if we want to know what it is to walk free and live up to our full potential, we should also look to Jesus. He was the freest person ever to walk this earth—and that is the way God wants us to live.

Jesus was free to be himself. . . . Although he was under tremendous pressure from his followers to become a different kind of messiah—a political, power-oriented, bread king for a chosen few—he rejected that role. He insisted upon fulfilling his real identity as the humble, serving, suffering Lord of all men and women, everywhere.

And so, when we are forgiven and when Christ lives within us, we throw off our identity handicaps along with our guilt. We reject the roles into which we have squeezed ourselves in our frantic attempts to win approval. We *are* approved—and we know it! We are free to become the persons God created us to be, free to touch and feel real life!

". . . I will give you a new heart—I will give you new and right desires—and put a new spirit within you. I will take out your stony hearts of sin and give you new hearts of love" (Ezekiel 36:26, Living Bible).

When we can love ourselves, we begin to feel worthy of achieving . . . and wonderful things happen. Talents which may have gone undiscovered, unnoticed, suddenly come to our attention once the Holy Spirit is given a free hand in our lives. Our imaginative powers are released from the bondage of our self-contempt—they literally soar! Our reasoning abilities become keener, our whole beings are more alert. We are moving toward our God-created potential.

Jesus was free to love others. . . . Unencumbered with undue concern for the self, Jesus was free to give himself to those around him, to meet them in a heartbeat-to-heartbeat relationship. People felt his interest and his love.

One of the most beautiful things God does for us with his love is to give us an appreciation of other people's right to be free. No longer will we want to manipulate or dominate or oppress or shape, even for the best of intentions. We will realize that we are dealing with others of God's creation who also have the right to be themselves.

Jesus was free to express his emotions. . . . He could love and let people know it. . . . He could allow the tears to fall at the death of a friend. . . . He had the freedom to be angry.

And we, when we are free, will live in reality rather than fantasy. As we feel life we will express our reactions to it— without embarrassment or shame. We will not be afraid to own our emotions . . . we will not fear conflict. Knowing that we can trust ourselves to communicate in love, we will not be afraid of close relationships.

Jesus was free to risk. . . . Secure in the love of his Father . . . and in the knowledge that he was about his Father's business, Jesus was able to take the ultimate risk of going into the city where he would be crucified.

So, we, too—as his people—will be free to take risks, to face the dangers of involvement in the real world where the action is taking place . . . and where we are very much needed.

Jesus was free to serve. . . . He was free to be vulnerable, to find common cause with the weak, the poor, and the oppressed.

If we accept God's love, it will awaken in us a compassion for all those who struggle against the odds in life. As we become free, we will want to serve—both God and those around us. . . . And we will do it in gratitude for all God has given us.

Jesus was free to live fully—to love God and enjoy him forever. . . . Sin and guilt separate us from God. It is Jesus, the Savior, who brings us back.

The most exciting news in the world is that Christ gives full and final forgiveness to anyone who is penitent in heart. He restores us to fellowship with God . . . and this is the meaning of a full life! This is our original destiny.

Christ not only points the way—he *is* the way. By his example, he shows us that our ultimate freedom is achieved in loving God and enjoying him forever. This is the life abundant . . . and it begins with forgiveness.

I started writing this book with a prayer, a prayer that

someone carrying a burden of guilt—a burden he or she was never meant to bear—would be moved to put the burden down . . . to let God do his work in that person's life. Perhaps that someone was you. If it was, then I want to close with another prayer especially for you. . . .

May you know fully the release from your burden, the joy of your forgiveness. And from this time on, may you walk free in Christ. For "if the Son makes you free, you will be free indeed" (John 8:32, RSV). Amen.